Tipton
A Third Selection

KEITH HODGKINS &
JOHN BRIMBLE

SUTTON PUBLISHING

Sutton Publishing Limited
Phoenix Mill · Thrupp · Stroud
Gloucestershire · GL5 2BU

First published 2001

Reprinted in 2002

Copyright © Keith Hodgkins & John
Brimble, 2001

Title page photograph: A Tipton Harriers
championship medal from the 1920s.

British Library Cataloguing in Publication Data
A catalogue record for this book is available from the
British Library.

ISBN 0-7509-2832-8

Typeset in 10.5/13.5 Photina.
Typesetting and origination by
Sutton Publishing Limited.
Printed and bound in England by
J.H. Haynes & Co. Ltd, Sparkford.

The 1919 Housing Act enabled local authorities to provide good quality housing with government subsidies and Tipton, in common with most other industrial towns, set about building estates to accommodate people displaced by the clearance of slum houses in older areas. One of the first developments of this kind in Tipton was built on the high ground bordering the Dudley to Wolverhampton line of the Great Western Railway and comprised Geneva Road, Cedar Road, Menin Road, Poplar Avenue, and Shrubbery Avenue. In this view of Shrubbery Avenue around 1930 a group of people gather around a motor lorry, no doubt eager to find out what is being delivered to one of their neighbours. At the top of the picture the boundary fence of the railway can be seen.

CONTENTS

A horse-drawn narrowboat heads towards Coseley Tunnel along Thomas Telford's New Main Line canal against the backdrop of Tipton's industrial skyline, in the 1920s. The Tipton UDC boundary lies beyond the high Wallbrook Bridge, which carries Old End over the canal. With the residential development of the area in the 1950s the road was renamed Central Avenue by Coseley UDC. To the right in the middle distance is the prominent profile of St Matthew's church, which towers above the multi-gabled factory of Bean's Engineering.

ACKNOWLEDGEMENTS

The authors are pleased to acknowledge the invaluable help given by the following friends and colleagues who have loaned photographs and supplied information.

John Allen, Colin Aston, Maurice Atkins, Mrs Atkins, Charlie Baker, Bill Bawden, Mrs Bettridge, Alf Breakwell, Marion Brennan, Ray Brothwood, Doris Bullock, Violet and Joshua Churchman, John Cooksey, Jack Corfield, Len Davies, Pat Davies, John Deane, David Dugmore, Alan Doggett, Zena Duffield, Jeremy Elwell, Janice Endean, Trevor Fletcher, Hilda Francis, Peter Glews, Joe Gripton, Phil Hill, Wally Hill, Una Hodgkins, J. Hooper, Jack Haugh, Mike Holloway, Jim Houghton, David Humphries, Paul Hunter, Gaynor Iddles, Pat Kendrick, Mrs J. Laight, E. Lakin, Jack and Lily Lloyd, David McDougal, Michael Mensing, Mrs E. Mills, Ron Moss, Clive Murray, Mrs Naylor, John Osborne, Borghildur Gudmundsdottir, M. Page, Harold Parton, Mrs Paskin, Chris Patterson, Alf Perks, Fred Perks, Mrs E. Pound, T.R. Preston, Alan Price, Terry Price, Jill Rhodes, Ken Rock, Frank Rogers, Beatrice Screen, Mr and Mrs Shelley, Mr Stacey, Bill Steventon, Ron Thomas, Kenneth Tibbetts, Mrs Torrington, Bob Trease, R. Trease, Janet Turner, Mrs Warmer, Mrs Watt, Ann Watton, Paul and Beryl Welch, Jean Weston, Vi Whetton, Dorothy Whitcombe, the late Ray Whitcombe, Barry Whitehouse, Harry Whitehouse, John Whitehouse, David Whyley, Brian Williams, Ned Williams, Margaret Willetts, David Wilson, Margaret and Terry Young.

We are also grateful to:
Birmingham Post and Mail, National Waterways Museum, Tipton Civic Society, Tipton and Coseley Building Society, Tipton Harriers, Sandwell Libraries, Sandwell Museums, South Staffordshire Water Co., Stafford Record Office, *Wolverhampton Express and Star*.

Special thanks to Jonathan Brimble for his help in preparing the book and, as always, to the editorial team at Sutton Publishing.

INTRODUCTION

Those of us who are interested in local history are constantly searching for evidence of what life was really like in the past. Photographs provide many of the answers, at least from the 1850s onwards, while contemporary prints and paintings give us some clues as to social styles and conventions. But we must also examine the works of various writers to gain an insight into the perceptions and attitudes of previous generations. One of the most prolific Black Country writers of a century ago was Frederick Hackwood (1851–1926) and we make no apology for opening our third book on Tipton with a revealing profile of our town contributed by Hackwood to the 1907 *Tipton and District Illustrated Annual*:

Tipton to the visitor is not an inviting spot; it is certainly bewildering if not exactly depressing. It labours under the disadvantage of being a widely scattered region. To all intents and purposes it consists of four separate distinct townships. Tipton proper, Great Bridge, Dudley Port and Princes End, all of them being on the outer border of the parish and enclosing as in a ring the remainder of its area.

There is no concentration, nor are the interests of the various manufacturing centres always identical; one part using its railway communications; another rejoicing in its canal facilities and yet another relying upon its main roads and tramway services. In addition to its railways and tramways, Tipton parish has no less than 30 miles of canals – has it not been styled as the 'Venice of the Black Country'? – whereby its surface is as much cut up as is the underground by its honeycomb of mines.

And yet many of the place names of the parish conjure up visions of a once pleasant landscape, whose pristine surface was varied by a village green that extended its borders into breezy heathlands; by undulations of hill and dale, by fruitful gardens and smiling pasture lands intersected by purling streams the imagination easily recalls the names Tipton Green and Horseley Heath. In Ocker Hill and Tividale; in Summerhill and Bloomfield; in the Lea Brook and the pastoral Sheepwash, that of yore could be seen by the wayfarer plodding his lonesome way across the old 'Greet Bridge'.

All these rural spots of reminiscence have vanished long ago, sacrificed to the interests of the plutocratic mine owner; nor can we find that he has left in their place, by way of compensation, any of the philanthropic establishments, those benevolent institutions by which the beneficially inclined do so much to ameliorate the conditions of life in crowded centres like the work-a-day world of modern Tipton.

How great is the havoc thus made on what was once a fair and smiling landscape may be judged by the view which yet obtains from the opposite side of the Castle Hill, where the virgin landscape still exists, untouched by the hand of the spoiler; serene woods and fields stretching away into the far horizon – Clent Hill in Worcestershire, and the Clee in Shropshire being prominent objects; some sharp eyes on a clear day even distinguishing the dim outline of the far-away hills on the Welsh border.

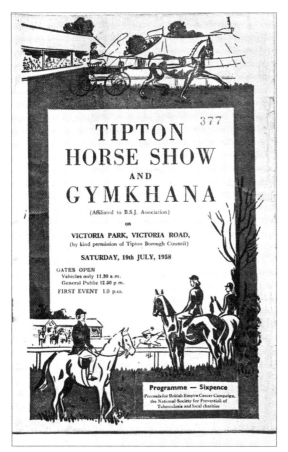

The programme for the 1958 Tipton Horse Show and Gymkhana.

Indeed the Tiptonian, like the true philosopher he is, consoles himself with the reflection that Dudley Castle, with its halo of Medieval romance, and the castle grounds with all their natural charms, are his to enjoy without let or hindrance. For are they not practically within his borders? Well, at the farthest they are only just beyond them and if he likes to extend his impropriation, he can take in the Wrens Nest Hill and then it is certain that he can confidently match his interesting bits of scenery, even against the beauties of 'wild Wales' in the distance.

But to return again to the heart of Tipton where its life is palpitating with the beat and throb of a thousand steam engines. Here in great profusion is the 'Metal of Mars' as Dud Dudley called it, in every shape and form, here is iron being manipulated and fashioned to the service of man in every conceivable way that human ingenuity can devise for (as saith Sir Thomas More in his *Utopia*) it is that metal 'without which man can no better live than without fire and water'.

Tipton owed all the desecration of its surface, all the desolation of its scenery to its almost inexhaustible stores of mineral wealth, for here was found iron ore lying invitingly side by side with the fuel and the flux wherewith to convert it into ready cash, here was fuel so cheap, plentiful and accessible that Capital felt itself compelled to cover the parish with furnaces, forges and foundries; and today the hammers of its countless mills and thudding forges are the actual 'Tipton Slashers' – striking a multitude of heavy blows, not to the damage of any human body but to the profit and advantage of the body politic.

In Tipton, Vulcan is everywhere supreme; and from the thousands of hearths that constitute his altars, never cease to arise columns of incense. To the Tiptonian, therefore, a smoke-laden sky is always regarded as the outward visible sign of the town's prosperity:

> They dread it not that stretch of smoke
> From Dudley Port to Wednesbury Oak.

From the distance afar, busy Tipton can never fail to be marked on the horizon by a pillar of smoke by day or a pillar of fire by night.

As to the enterprise and ability with which the iron has been dealt with, it is to be reckoned no mean achievement for a town situated as Tipton is, in the very heart and centre of the land, and as far distant in every direction as it can be from our seaboard, that it should take upon itself to supply anchors, cables and chains to those whose business it is, 'to go down to the deep sea in ships'.

And the exceptional facilities for the transport of merchandises and manufactures which Tipton possesses in its railways and waterways promise even greater developments in the future; as witness the recent advent of such important industrial corporations as the Mond Gas Works and the Midlands Electric Supply establishment. It remains only for a wise governing body, whilst encouraging such enterprises, to lose no opportunities for the improvement of the place to let in as much sweetness and light as possible – their new public park is a most laudable effort in this direction – and to neglect nothing that will make for the material, moral and intellectual advancement of the inhabitants.

For industrially, Tipton has been found a land overflowing, not with 'milk and honey' but with coal and iron; and it cannot be denied that in this busy Land of Promise the best has been made of both. Long may Tipton flourish.

These words were written almost a century ago and although the coal and iron industries have vanished, they have produced a great legacy of achievement for the town. Many of Hackwood's sentiments still apply today and Tipton is cherished by its inhabitants, not as a postcard village but as a hardworking town with a pride in its past.

The view looking north in 1958 from the recently completed Coronation House flats reveals Tipton's industrial skyline dominated by the Town gasworks, centre, and the Mond gasworks to the right. Prominent in the middle distance is the gable of Canal Street Methodist chapel demolished in 1973, while in the foreground is Round's timber yard and Coronation Gardens, opened alongside the Old Main Line canal in June 1953. These gardens were one of the first developments in the Black Country to acknowledge the amenity value of the canal system although sadly the example was not followed with any enthusiasm for another two or three decades.

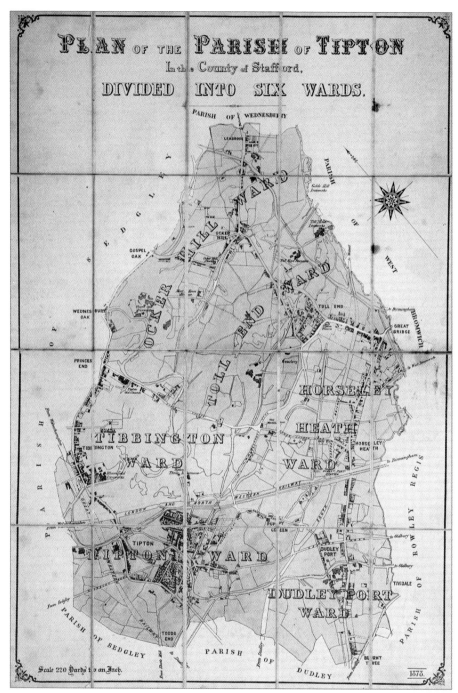

The Tipton parish map of 1878 showing the six wards that existed at the time. These had increased to eight by the 1930s to cater for the rising population. Despite the date, the map seems to be based on an earlier survey, as the Princes End branch railway which opened in 1863 is not shown and the three other lines which served the town, each of which was operating by 1852, are shown only as parcels, as if under construction. This suggests that the map is based on Fowler's survey of 1849. The actual size of the map is 28in by 18½in (355mm by 235mm).

1

Civic Life

Arthur Frederick Welch was born in 1883 within the sound of Bow bells but soon afterwards moved to the Black Country. Shortly before his seventeenth birthday he lost his left eye in an accident at the Vono works. He was to marry Minnie Smith, a woman who was proficient at needlework, and by 1918 they had started a drapery business at Great Bridge. Mr Welch was elected to Tipton Urban District Council in 1925 and in 1938 had the honour of being the Charter Mayor when Tipton became a borough. Mrs Welch became the Charter Mayoress.

From 1877 until 1935 the local government of Tipton was operated from the Public Offices in Owen Street near the railway station. The headquarters was transferred to the new offices in Sedgley Road West (known as the Municipal Buildings) and on 7 March 1935, the new buildings were opened by the Rt Hon. Arthur Greenwood MP. The new council chamber had a round-ended table for the council members and a raised dais for the chairman (later the mayor).

When Tipton received its Charter 1938, its civic regalia was presented to the town by a group local industrialists. Dominated by the large mace, the regalia has been laid out in the Council Chamber at the Municipal Buildings. Here are the chains of office, silver, ebony and ivory gave silver gilt loving cup, silver tea set and tray and silver casket which houses an engrossed record of subscribers and the presentation. On the wall is the Borough coat o arms as presented by the schoolchildren of Tipton. When Tipton Borough disbanded the chains of office, along with those the Borough of Wednesbury, were put on display at West Bromwich Town Hall but, in 1981, the Tipto Mayor and Mayoress's chains wer stolen in a smash and grab robber

After a long fight, Tipton eventually became a municipal borough and on 1 October 1938 the Charter of Incorporation was presented to the Charter Mayor, Councillor A.F. Welch, by the Rt Hon. the Earl of Harrowby, Lord Lieutenant of the County of Stafford. The Earl is seen here handing over the documents to the Mayor, watched by the Mayoress and by the Deputy Charter Mayor, Councillor W.J.W. George. The mace adds civic dignity to the occasion.

On 7 June 1997 the Victoria Park Steering Group organised a celebration to mark the centenary of the park. At this event the Mayor of Sandwell, Councillor W. Melia, together with a group of children from St Martin's School, buried a time capsule near the Victorian drinking fountain. This had been donated by the Dudley Port Rolling Mills and contained, among other items, a history of the park. Councillor Melia is seen with the mace bearer, Mr Tom Dale, who proudly displays the magnificent Tipton Borough Council mace.

The members of the Tipton Urban District Council under the chairmanship of Joseph Powell JP pose at the rear of the Public Offices in Owen Street in 1911. This was the fourth year that Councillor Powell had held the office of chairman, having previously held the post between 1905 and 1908. He was the most prominent figure in Tipton's local government at the time, having also held the prestigious position of chairman of the education committee in 1909.

The officers of the Tipton Urban District Council sit for an official photograph outside the Public Offices in Owen Street with the clerk to the council, Mr J.H. Stockdale, centre front, in 1911. Also in this picture can be seen John Parkes, who in 1915 wrote a *History of Tipton* (extreme left, front row).

The visit to Tipton by Princess Marie Louise of Schleswig-Holstein in 1909 was the first ever royal visit to the town. It created so much interest and excitement that crowds turned out in their hundreds to witness the occasion. The photograph shows the Princess in her carriage on Victoria Park drawn up close to the bandstand, which had been decorated with streamers and bunting for the occasion. Most of the onlookers it appears had dressed in their Sunday best clothing.

A group from the 1st Tipton Boy Scouts at a gathering, probably in Victoria Park. The seated figure dressed in military uniform is Major John Norton Griffiths, MP for the Wednesbury division of which Tipton was then part. The Scouts' commissioner for the South Staffordshire division, because of his political views he was affectionately known as 'Empire Jack'.

Inspector Burgess and Sergeant Snead sit outside Tipton police station in Lower Church Lane with the
complement of constables, around 1910. Tipton's rather gaunt looking police station was built in 1864 of local bl
brick. Just out of the picture, the Staffordshire 'knot' overlooks the front door. Tipton magistrates' courts sat he
until the amalgamation with West Bromwich in 1966. The notice on the wall behind PC Reynolds offers a reward

An election pamphlet proposes Arthur Frederick Welch
for the Staffordshire County Council triennial elections
held on 6 March 1934. Welch polled 1,392 votes against
his opponent Arthur Edward Bannister's 843 and was
duly elected as a county councillor for the Horseley Heath
Division. The pamphlet was printed and published by the
local Great Bridge printer, Blackham's.

In recognition of 40 years' service with the Tipton Fire Brigade, Mr A.G. Batten was presented with a beautiful oak secretaire by the Mayor, Councillor A.F. Welch, on 6 April 1937. Mr Batten joined the Tipton Brigade in 1896 and worked his way up to become Chief Officer in 1937. In 1920 he was decorated with the OBE for his gallant rescue services during the Zeppelin raids of 1916.

The Lord Lieutenant of Staffordshire, the earl of Harrowby and the countess visit Tipton on a tour of inspection of Civil Defence services, October 1940. The entourage was met by Councillor Welch and the town clerk, Mr K.W. Madin. First stop was the headquarters of the Tipton company of the Home Guard, followed by the Fire Brigade headquarters in Albion Street and thence to the library in Victoria Road. Here the 'Mobile Casualty Unit', a veritable hospital on wheels, was inspected. The earl and countess were impressed by this, which had been a gift to the town by the Palethorpe brothers.

'Another priceless jewel for Tipton' was how the local press announced the opening of the new park at Ocker Hill. This was the realisation of a 25-year dream when an area of pit banks and marl holes was turned into a public open space. Originally called Ocker Hill Park, it was later renamed Jubilee Park to commemorate the silver jubilee of the King and Queen. Here the park is being officially opened on 13 April 1935 by the chairman of the council, Councillor A.F Welch, watched by Councillor W.E. Hampton, chairman of the Parks and Baths committee. The interested onlookers are K.W. Madin, clerk to the council, and H.N. Woodward, surveyor.

The opening of Jubilee Park was regarded as a great new asset to Tipton. It was greeted with comments such as 'wilderness made to bloom like a rose' and 'boon to mothers, delight to children and paradise for sports lovers'. So important was the occasion that the opening was attended by almost every member of Tipton Urban District Council, proud of their town's new possession. The members are seen here surrounding the chairman, Councillor Welch.

The golden ceremonial key used by Councillor A.F. Welch to officially open Jubilee Park was inscribed on both sides with details of the event. The key still survives as a treasured possession of the Welch family. It made a return visit to the park in 1999 on the occasion of the unveiling of a blue plaque to commemorate the original opening in 1935.

One of the activities of Tipton Civic Society since its formation in 1988 has been to erect plaques in commemoration of important people and events in the town's history. The Jubilee Park plaque was unveiled on 11 September 1999, most appropriately by Paul Welch, right, grandson of Councillor Arthur Welch, who performed the original opening ceremony in 1935 and became Tipton's first mayor. Also in attendance was Barry Whitehouse, son of Tipton's last mayor, Councillor Jonah Whitehouse. These two men were thus representing a unique historical link with the period of Tipton's borough status from 1938 to 1966. Paul Welch is holding the 1935 ceremonial key which was presented to his grandfather.

Charles F. Clifton, the Tipton Borough mace bearer, opens the door of the mayoral Humber car in 1950 as the mayoress, Mrs Hampton, steps out. Mrs Hampton was the wife of Alderman William Edward Hampton, who held the office of mayor of Tipton from 1947 to 1950.

The civic remembrance service held around the cenotaph in Victoria Park, November 1956, led by the vicar of Tipton, Revd A.W.C. Thomas and attended by the mayor, Alderman James Gill and the local Member of Parliament for Rowley Regis and Tipton, Arthur Henderson. The music was provided by the Tipton Salvation Army band.

On 24 June 1994 the first ever visit to Tipton by Her Majesty Queen Elizabeth II attracted massive crowds to Owen Street to catch a glimpse of her as she travelled from the railway station, having arrived on the royal train. Here she is seen with her entourage passing the Tipton and Coseley Building Society offices en route to a reception at the Tipton City Challenge offices in High Street.

On arrival at Partnership House the Queen was greeted by Mr Colin Cooke, Chairman of the Tipton Challenge Partnership and Miss Betty Boothroyd, Speaker of the House of Commons and Member of Parliament for West Bromwich West, of which Tipton forms part. Her Majesty unveiled a plaque in the building to commemorate the visit.

Standing in Tipton cemetery on 11 September 1994 is the mayor of Sandwell, Councillor J. Padden, following the service of re-dedication of the memorial to 19 young girls killed by an explosion at Dudley Port on 6 March 1922. They died while they were working at breaking up miniature rifle cartridges and were aged between only 13 and 15 years. This event caused outrage and the memorial was erected by public subscription. The monument became worn and after calls by Tipton Civic Society and others for its renovation the Council took action to restore it.

Neptune Health Park, opened in 1999, was built on the site of Wright's Neptune Chain and Anchor Works and appropriately took as its emblem an anchor. To celebrate the chain and anchor industries of this part of the town, Tipton Civic Society erected an anchor on a brick plinth, which was dedicated at a special ceremony on 26 March 2000, conducted by Revd Pat Davies. Among those attending were His Worship the Mayor of Sandwell, Councillor John Edwards, chairman of the Tipton Civic Society, Ray Brothwood and other members of that group. On the other side of the building is a commemorative plaque outlining the activities of Wright's forge.

2

Tipton Green

John Henry Stockdale was born in York in 1865 and in 1887 became a solicitor. He moved to the Black Country and started to practise in Wednesbury in 1889. He took an interest in public life and became a member of Wednesbury Borough Council. When John M. Waring, the long-serving clerk to local government in Tipton, retired in 1905 he was succeeded by Mr Stockdale, who became a household name in Tipton and held the position until 1927. Stockdale Parade was named after him.

An early view of Victoria Park, soon after its opening in 1901. Rowing boats can be seen on the pool, while in the background is the parkkeeper's lodge with the building known as Holbeche opposite. Beyond these is the newly developed housing estate known as The Terraces, the gasworks and railway line with goods wagons. In the park itself are greenhouses for growing the park plants and to their right is an open structure, apparently an aviary. Older residents recall seeing peafowl there.

The cenotaph, a granite obelisk erected in a prominent position on Victoria Park. It was unveiled on 24 August 1921 by the Marquis of Cambridge, who was patron of the Midland Counties area of the Royal British Legion. To the original gold inscription of '1914–1919 The Great War', was added '1939–1945 The World War'. Other inscriptions are 'Honoured for Evermore', 'Our Glorious Dead' and 'Resurgam Laus Deo'.

The ornamental drinking fountain near the entrance gates to Victoria Park was presented by Mr John Monninton Waring and his wife in 1903 to commemorate their golden wedding. It also marks 50 years of public service given to the people of Tipton by Mr Waring as council clerk. The cast iron umbrella with heron motifs is a design by Walter McFarlane & Co. of Glasgow. This 1960s picture shows the original fountainhead, which has since been removed. The structure is now a listed building.

Randalls Lane was renamed Victoria Road in about 1900 when the public park was laid out to mark the long reign of Queen Victoria. This view of *c.* 1910 shows the main gates to the park, gaslit and flanked by the mock-timbered keeper's lodge, which had been erected by a local builder named Gittins. Opposite is the house named Avoca, the home of Richard Hancock, a Labour member of Tipton Council for several years. The garden of the house was surrounded by a cinder wall. Hidden by the trees is Holbeche, owned by John Parkes, the Tipton local historian, which later became a nursing home.

The 1930 Tipton Carnival Queen, her attendants and the carnival committee pose for a photograph on Victoria Park following the crowning ceremony, which took place on the bandstand. The Queen, Miss Sherwood, with her ladies in waiting Beatrice Wheale and Ethel Ball, was crowned by Mrs Williams, the wife of Dr N.V. Williams (on the Queen's right). During the ceremony Mrs Williams presented the Queen with a gold wristlet watch, the ladies in waiting with shingle sets and the trainbearers with boxes of chocolates. In the centre of the front row of officials is Councillor S. Davies.

The minister of Park Lane Methodist chapel, Revd Arfon Roberts, watches Miss F. Sherwood and Mrs Chatwin cut a cake produced by the local bakers, Hurley's, to celebrate the centenary of the building in 1966. Known locally as the 'cathedral' of Tipton Methodism, the old chapel was designed by the Wolverhampton architect George Bidlake, and officially opened on 25 September 1866 by Revd William Arthur, president of the Wesleyan Methodist Conference.

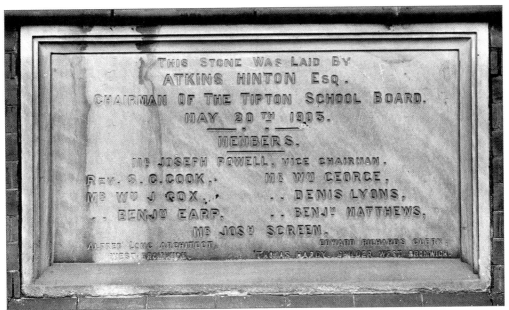

THIS STONE WAS LAID BY
ATKINS HINTON Esq.
CHAIRMAN OF THE TIPTON SCHOOL BOARD.
MAY 20 TH 1903.
MEMBERS.
MR JOSEPH POWELL, VICE CHAIRMAN.
REV. S. G. COOK, MR WM GEORGE,
MR WM J COX, DENIS LYONS,
BENJN EARP, BENJN MATTHEWS,
MR JOSH SCREEN.
ALFRED LONG ARCHITECT, EDWARD RICHARDS CLERK
WEST BROMWICH. THOMAS HARDY BUILDER WEST BROMWICH

Tipton School Board was established in 1871 with William Hipkins as its first chairman. The Board erected seven schools, the last being at Park Lane. The foundation stone for this was laid on 20 May 1903 by the last chairman, Mr Atkins Hinton, who was the sub postmaster in Owen Street. The stone also relates that Edward Richards was clerk to the School Board at the time and that the architect was Alfred Long of New Street, West Bromwich. The builder was Thomas Hardy of West Bromwich. The school was demolished in 1992 and the stone is now preserved at the Alexandra High School. The nine member School Board met at the Public Offices in Owen Street on the first Thursday each month.

With Park Lane Methodist chapel in the background, West Bromwich council officials inspect the site of the new Birch Street health centre, 1 May 1970. The centre was built as an extension to the 1950s clinic to provide accommodation for the practice of Dr J. Milligan. It was opened by Sir Keith Joseph, Secretary of State for Health and Social Services on 5 April 1971 but became obsolete in 1999 after the opening of the Neptune Health Park. The site has since been developed for housing, taking the name Cathedral Close in recognition of the nearby chapel.

A ship's mooring swivel made at the Castle Street works of H.P. Parkes and Co. for the Dreadnought class battleship *Orion*, launched on 20 August 1910. The ship displaced 22,220 tons, had a complement of 753 and was in service until 1922. Parkes had achieved early fame in 1866 when the company manufactured a replacement anchor for Brunel's steamship *Great Eastern*, being at the time the largest anchor ever made. The achievement is commemorated by a Tipton Civic Society blue plaque on the Castle Street site.

A view of Castle Road looking towards Dudley Road in the first decade of the twentieth century, long before the south side of the street was developed. In the distance the large house with tall chimneys is Ivy House, the home of Mr Daniel Hipkins JP, who owned the soap and candle manufactory at Bloomfield. Mr Hipkins was a leading figure in the town at the turn of the century, difficult years which saw large-scale changes in local government and the decline of the iron trade. He guided Tipton through these as chairman of the local Board of Health from 1889 to 1894, and then as chairman of the Urban District Council for six terms of office between 1895 and 1902.

Seen here in the garden of Ivy House is the wedding party of Miss Ethel Mary Hipkins and Revd Walter J. Morgan, 9 August 1911. Miss Hipkins was a daughter of Daniel Hipkins who can be seen seated on the extreme left of the front row. By desire of the families the wedding was a quiet affair though the happy pair were the recipients of many hearty good wishes and some exquisite presents.

Owen Street in the early days of its decline, late 1950s. Still to be seen was the Post Office on the right, with a year or two of its life remaining prior to its relocation to Union Street (see p. 38). Frank Jones, the drapers and, in the distance, the Regal cinema were still standing. Southans Bros the furnishers are seen on the left and, in the foreground, the Fountain Inn. Note that several of the shops still have sunblinds.

On 28 July 1961 a large pressure vessel slipped from the low loader that was transferring it from Wright's For[g] and Engineering Co. As the vehicle turned from Factory Road into Owen Street, a manoeuvre necessary to avo[id] the restricted bridges at the other end of Factory Road and at the top of Owen Street. . .

. . . the vessel rolled across the road into the frontage of the Co-op store, inflicting considerable damage, although luckily no one was hurt. The Co-op eventually moved to a new supermarket in Stockdale Parade in 1980, after which the ol[d] store was demolished along with most of the rest of Owen Street.

Landlord William Vaughan stands outside the Fountain Inn, Owen Street, late 1920s. The pub was still in its original three-storeyed condition and sold Samuel Allsopp's mild and bitter ales from Burton on Trent. A sign on the bar window denotes that musical evenings could be enjoyed here. The notice on the corner is a timetable for Midland Red omnibus services, which began running through Owen Street in the mid-1920s.

Two doors down from the Fountain Inn at 53 Owen Street was the shop of R.B. Bramford which in the 1920s catered for all the writing and stationery requirements of the inhabitants of Tipton Green. Swan fountain pens, envelopes, postcards, pen nibs, writing paper and a wide range of books were on sale. Bramford also had another shop at 2 Bell Street, Tipton.

A Walsall bus on the 865 route (facing the camera) passes a Dudley-bound Midland Red on the 265 route in Owen Street between St Paul's church and the Regal cinema in 1955. The 265 Dudley to Walsall bus route began in 1949 under the joint operation of Walsall Corporation and Midland Red. By 1951 the 865 service through to Stafford had been added, alternating half hourly with the 265.

By the mid-1970s, following the formation of the West Midlands Passenger Transport Executive and their subsequent takeover of the Midland Red services, the 865 was withdrawn and the 265 re-numbered as the 301, which became known jokingly as the 'darters' bus. In the summer of 1977 a former Walsall Corporation bus, repainted in West Midlands livery, heads a 301 along Owen Street, having just passed the Black Cock pub at the junction with Union Street.

The Regal cinema in Owen Street showed its last film, *Jazz Boat*, starring Anthony Newley, on Saturday 3 December 1960. Mr David Duckworth, whose family had owned the premises since 1922, was reported in the *Tipton Herald* as blaming a 'higher standard of living' for the decline of the cinema industry. On the last night the cinema's usherettes prepare for their final customers.

'Tipton Vics' FC at the rear of the Black Cock pub in Owen Street, 1955 or 1956. The club was re-established in 1953 after attaining eminence in local league circles before the war. The original Tipton Victoria FC won the Dudley Guest Hospital Charity Cup in 1900. Back row, left to right: F. Poulton, G. Bunch, D. Bown, E. Barlow, A. Plested, F. Street, J. Pickerill (manager). Front row: B. Pickerill, J. Edwards, B. Styles, T. Woodcock, H. Stott. The team played their home matches on Victoria Park.

Born in Dudley in 1856 of Irish parents, Denis Lyons came to Tipton in 1879 and soon began to take an interest in public life. He became a member of the old School Board and Local Board of Health and was for some years an active member of the Urban District Council. He was totally involved in local matters, being one of those people who has his finger in every pie. In business he founded a large boot and leather undertaking in Owen Street. His Irish descent may have been responsible for a fund of natural wit to which at times he gave free vent, to the delight of his colleagues.

On a January morning in 1969 the build-up of traffic in Owen Street behind the West Bromwich Corporation refuse vehicle suggests that the railway crossings are closed. A familiar situation that has long frustrated local motorists, the problem is due to be alleviated in 2006 with the planned construction of an underpass. In the distance a Midland Red bus on the 272 service from Sedgley to Great Bridge waits to turn right into Union Street and, on the left of the street, the once familiar façade of the Midland Bank is prominent, standing above the distinctive raised pavement.

St Paul's Church of England Junior and Infants Schools as seen on 15 April 1970 were built in 1874, enlarged in 1899 and accommodated over 200 children. In 1994 the schools were relocated to a site a short distance away across the railway lines. The old buildings were demolished and St Paul's Community Centre (including Tipton Heritage Centre) opened on the site in 1996. To the left of the picture is the gable end of the Noah's Ark public house, whose licensee in the 1950s and '60s was Tom Cartwright, a noted local boxer.

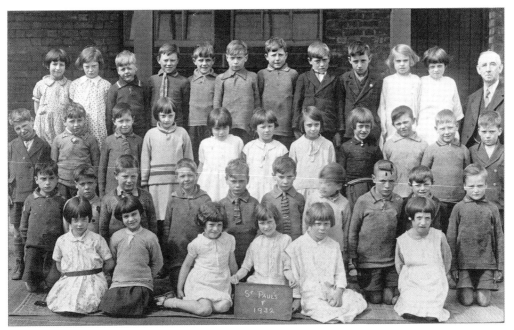

A group of pupils of St Paul's School, Wood Street, pose for a photograph with their headmaster Mr Samuel Murray in 1932. Mr Murray was appointed in 1919 and succeeded another well-known figure, Mr Samuel Kelsall.

British Waterways workmen are replacing the bottom gate of lock no. 2 on the Toll End Communication canal in the early 1950s, with the aid of shear legs. This lock was situated on the north side of the bridge carrying Alexandra Road over the canal adjacent to the Lockerbie and Wilkinson factory. The Toll End canal was built as two separate branches, linked in 1809 to form a through route of 1½ miles from Toll End Junction on the Walsall Canal to Tipton Green Junction on the Birmingham Canal. The houses visible in the distance are those in Thursfield Road, Little Burton.

Tipton railway station, named Tipton Owen Street for a time between 1950 and 1968, was opened on 1 July 1852 by the London and North Western Railway as part of the Stour Valley route between Wolverhampton and Birmingham. The Stour Valley name, although still in use, is an historical anomaly owing to an unrealised early proposal to build a branch line from Smethwick to Stourport. The late nineteenth-century brick built ticket office photographed here in 1964 lost its protective canopy in the run-up to electrification of the line in 1967.

A Bangor to Birmingham New Street train powered by Britannia class locomotive 70033 *Charles Dickens* approaches Watery Lane crossing having just passed through Tipton Owen Street station, Sunday 30 July 1961. To the right of the picture is Alexandra Road and the bridge over the Toll End Communication canal which also passes beneath the railway at a point indicated by girders between the tracks, level with the fourth carriage of the train.

Taken on the same day as the previous picture, this view from Watery Lane in the opposite direction towards Dudley Port reveals a panorama of semaphore signals with the Tipton Town gasworks and the Mond gasworks flanking the north side of the railway as a diesel parcels railcar passes by.

By 1978 the scene was quite different, with the old gasworks replaced by the new naphtha plant. The railway had also been modernised, and yet, incredibly, the old crossing gates and gas lighting remained intact. The gates were rarely used and could only be seen in the open position on occasional Sundays when the line was out of use for maintenance purposes. The gas lamps survived until about 1980 and the gates remained until the right of way was extinguished in 1992, depriving Tiptonians of an historic and very useful pedestrian route.

til the early 1960s boats delivering coal from the Cannock coalfield to Black Country wharfs and factories were
amiliar scene in Tipton. Here a pair of boats head towards Watery Lane bridge on the New Main Line canal on
nisty morning in 1953 having just passed the junction with the now defunct Toll End Communication canal.

oking west from the picture above this March 1969 telephoto shot across the roofs of houses in Waterloo Street
wards the dominant spire of Park Lane Methodist chapel graphically illustrates the reason for this place of
orship becoming known as Tipton's 'cathedral' of Methodism. Further in the distance peering over Castle Hill is
e intrusive profile of Dudley's Eve Hill flats.

The old Union Street consisted of nineteenth-century houses and shops. A redevelopment scheme w
implemented in 1959 to provide these new flats and shops, which included a new Post Office to replace the
premises at 40 Owen Street. One of the oldest buildings to survive this planning phase was the former Globe I
which can be seen at the end of the new buildings.

In or about 1830 the Congregationalists began to
assemble for worship in a private house in Canal
Street. These were probably people with Welsh
origins. They continued to worship there until 183
and in 1840 the Ebenezer chapel was erected at th
top end of Union Street. The industrialist family of
Addenbrookes were long associated with the churc.
In 1867 Mr Clement of the Opera House, Dudley,
held a French class there. The old chapel was
demolished in 1964 as part of the Union Street
redevelopment.

A new market for Tipton. The new market in Union Street was officially opened on 1 June 1973 by Alderman Sid Martin, mayor of West Bromwich. In the late nineteenth century a market hall stood at the rear of the Fire Station in Albion Street, close to this site.

Joseph Richard Baker, better known as Joey, was one of the more colourful characters to have sat on Tipton Council. He set up his own hardware business at 42 Bell Street, tramping the streets selling his goods and becoming a popular local figure. He was elected to the council in 1907 and served until 1937, attaining the high office of chairman in 1932. In January 1933 he had the honour of opening the new swimming baths, having originally raised the issue of constructing the baths way back in 1909. He had long been an advocate of incorporation for Tipton, but sadly it came too late and he was never to sit on the Borough Council. His name is perpetuated in Baker Street.

The Queen's Head at 40 Bell Street, pictured in the 1930s when the licensee was Fanny Parkes. The pub closed in the 1950s and the building was converted to flats. Demolition took place in the mid-1960s.

From the 1850s to the advent of the Welfare State many public houses ran Sick and Dividend Societies, which enabled investors to withdraw money when unable to work through illness. The payment of interest on the clubs' savings was a legal requirement and this was paid in the form of checks or tokens, in denominations of one penny to sixpence, which could be spent in the pub, thus giving the licensee an incentive to administer his Society. Surviving pub checks give a fascinating insight into this long forgotten aspect of social history. These examples from Tipton Green show the Coach & Horses, Dudley Road, still open; the Beehive, Elliot Road, closed 1978; Old King's Head, Dudley Road, closed mid-1970s; Rose and Crown, Watery Lane (since renamed Walton Street then Queen's Road), still open; Albion Inn, Owen Street, closed 1978.

On 28 November 1939, brewers Butler's opened a public house on the Birmingham New Road in honour of Tipton having just been created a Borough. Christened the Tipton Arms, it was designed by local architects Scott and Clark. Appropriately it had as its sign the Borough of Tipton coat of arms. The pub closed in November 1994 to make way for a housing development with the name Tipps-Stone Close. This is a reference to one of the features on the Tipton coat of arms and was suggested by Tipton Civic Society.

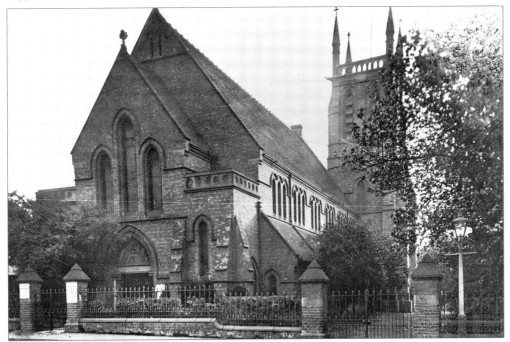

A factional disagreement at St Paul's church in Owen Street in 1875 led to St Matthew's church being built on Dudley Road in 1876. The approximate cost of the building was £6,000, of which the major benefactors were Sir Horace St Paul, the local landowner-industrialist, and the two Roberts brothers of Tipton Green Furnaces. It was built to plans by J.H. Gibbons of Birmingham.

The pathway at the rear of St Matthew's church shaded by trees presents a scene of rural tranquillity amidst the industry at the beginning of the twentieth century. From here fields stretched for some distance in the direction of Sedgley. It was in this area that the historic Green House was located.

Known as the Green House or Tipton Green Hall, this old building stood close to where St Matthew's church now stands. A timbered building of some antiquity, it was the home at one time of Edward Dudley, yeoman and a captain with Cromwell's army. The Civil War skirmish of 12 June 1644 known as the Battle of Tipton Green, in which Edward Dudley participated, took place in the fields around the house and to the east. The original house was still standing in 1798, when it was shaded by a grove of trees. Another house was erected there in the nineteenth century. It had several owners and was last used in 1868 as an academy.

Although the identity of the boys and the story behind the photograph is unknown, the location of this delightful study can be accurately pinpointed. It was taken opposite St Matthew's vicarage in Dudley Road looking towards Five Ways, probably in the first decade of the twentieth century. The house on the left is 113 Dudley Road, beyond which in the distance is Tipton's Great Western railway station, a view later blocked by the construction of council houses in the 1920s. The boy on the left clutches a bottle, while the other holds a billycan and, in his right hand, what appears to be a yo-yo. They look too young to be on their way to work; what were they up to?

A view of Dudley Road in the 1920s in the direction of Dudley, looking towards the position where the two boys in the picture above were standing. The precise spot can be identified by the pyramidal gate piers which, together with most of this row, were demolished in the late 1970s. The tram poles indicate that this was part of the Wednesbury to Dudley tram route.

The 7.15pm train from Stourbridge Junction to Wolverhampton Low Level approaches Tipton Five Way station, viewed from the footbridge which linked the top of Menin Road to the Foxyards, Whit Monday, 11 June 1962. In the background are the houses Shrubbery Avenue seen in the previous photograph and the long, tree-clad profile of Dudley's Castle Hill. Passenger trains on this route were withdrawn seven weeks later on 30 July.

Sedgley Road as seen about 1905 with its row of Edwardian villa type houses on the left hand side. These houses were quite opulent for the time and it became the desirable place to live in Tipton. As a result the houses were owned by several of Tipton's leading businessmen.

Sedgley Road (now with West added to the name) in the 1930s. On the left hand side more modern houses have been added to the original Edwardian villas. On the right hand side are the offices of Bean Cars Ltd, built during the First World War, which in 1935 were to become Tipton's Municipal Building.

At the beginning of the twentieth century William Bates offered home brewed ales, Guinness and bottled stout together with good stabling at his Five Ways Inn on the corner of Hurst Lane and Sedgley Road East. The entrance to the stables was the gateway on the extreme left. This building was replaced in 1923 by a new pub which was later renamed the Doughty Arms after Councillor William Doughty, the chairman of the Licensing Committee. In 1987 it was bought by Mad O'Rourke and transformed into the Pie Factory, now famed for its 'Desperate Dan Cow Pies'.

The Boatmen's Mission standing near the factory locks gave physical and spiritual sustenance to the boat people and their families. It was constructed in 1892 by the Incorporated Seamen and Boatmen's Friendly Society with financial assistance from the local landowner, the Earl of Dudley. The foundation stone was dedicated 'to the glory of God and for the good of the souls of those who pass on the canal'. On Sundays, church services were held at the mission and the nearby wharves in the hope of luring the boatmen away from the pubs. Since 1955 the building has been used for industrial purposes and the entrance from the canal, surmounted by a cross, has disappeared.

In the days of commercial carrying canal boats would pay tolls based on the weight of the cargo carried. This would be calculated from how deep the boat sat in the water, each toll office having a record of the number of 'dry inches' to tonnage carried for every registered boat. In order to formulate these tables each boat when new would be gauged by loading with known weights to record the displacement. This process was undertaken by the BCN Company in this gauging house, built in 1878 adjacent to the top of Factory Locks and seen here in 1957. The building was listed in 1974, unfortunately too late to prevent the poorly designed extension, which appears below.

Alan 'Caggy' Stevens (1918–97) was the last of the old school of Black Country working boatmen, having come from an Oldbury canal family, and spent all his working life on the cut. He established a boatyard on the old Watery Lane interchange basin in Tipton in 1978 and became known as a regular in the Noah's Ark pub in Wood Street in the 1980s and '90s. He was photographed in 1983 steering his tug *Caggy* into Factory top lock with the boat gauging station in the background.

3

Ocker Hill & Toll End

Arthur Edward Bannister, born in 1887, was a member of an old Ocker Hill family and spent most of his life in that part of Tipton. He worked as a boot and shoe repairer-cum-estate agent but was well known in the community as a church organist and churchwarden at St Mark's church. He gained a seat on Tipton District Council in 1913 and sat as a member for several years, becoming chairman in 1931. He also served the community as a magistrate. He was well known locally as a fine swimmer; for some years he was connected with Wednesbury Swimming Club, winning the Thomas Cup (100 yds) on two occasions. It seemed highly appropriate that when the foundation stone of Tipton's new baths was laid on 28 April 1932, he should have had the pleasure of carrying out the ceremony. His name is perpetuated in Bannister Road.

A Royal Scot class locomotive heads a mixed freight train on to the Princes End Branch, *c*. 1960. The train is just about to cross the invisible boundary between the boroughs of Wednesbury and Tipton, which followed the course of the Lea brook. The landscape, dominated by Ocker Hill power station, was to change dramatically in the 1980s and '90s following the demolition of the cooling towers and the construction of the Black Country spine road, which opened up this vast tract of previously inaccessible land for development.

The view along Leabrook Road towards Ocker Hill in August 1968 reveals the Britannia public house and the works of Prodorite Ltd, which since 1925 had specialised in the production of corrosion resistant industrial applications. In the distance on the canal bridge is the Bush pub, the only building in the picture to survive into the twenty-first century. The Britannia and its adjacent houses were demolished in the mid-1970s, followed by the Prodorite works in the 1980s, after which the land behind underwent an opencast coal operation prior to the construction of the Black Country spine road which subsequently relieved Leabrook Road of much of its through traffic.

The Post Office in a converted semi-detached house at 62 Leabrook Road just before the demolition of the houses on the corner of Willingsworth Road, May 1969. The houses have been fly-posted with attractions at Wednesbury Town Hall, Brierley Hill Civic Hall and Danilo, together with an election poster for the Wednesbury Market ward. The Post Office closed in the 1970s and the building became a newsagents and general store.

A BR class 25 diesel locomotive runs down the Princes End branch towards Wednesbury having just crossed the Walsall canal, May 1969. In the background stands the Leabrook works of John Bagnall and Sons Ltd, an old established firm of ironworkers which by this time was a subsidiary of F.H. Lloyd Holdings Ltd, specialising in the re-coiling of steel strip. The site became part of the opencast coal operation in the early 1990s.

The Gospel Oak public house marks a place where John Wesley is said to have preached the gospels during his visits to the Black Country in the eighteenth century. Seen here in September 1968 it is better known as Mother Shipton's, taking this name from a Mrs Emma Shipton who was landlady in the 1920s. The Shipton family also owned a farm in the locality. The name Gospel Oak originates from a stopping place in the ancient custom of 'beating the bounds' or walking the parish boundaries.

The three postwar cooling towers of the power station at Ocker Hill once dominated the view all around. Seen from Gospel Oak Road, they overshadowed the old Victorian board school with its Italianate tower, the Crown & Cushion public house and Gittins' 'little wooden shop'. This photograph was taken in September 1957.

In 1969 it was announced that Ocker Hill Junior School would be demolished to make way for a new school to house infants. Seen here is Mr Cyril Archer, a former pupil, looking at the foundation stone of the old school with his son, local Member of Parliament Peter Archer, now Lord Archer of Sandwell. Looking on is the headmaster Mr John Adams. The stone records that it was laid on 28 August 1899 by the chairman of the Tipton School Board, John Webb Esq.

A Sunday-service Birmingham to Stafford diesel train passes the site of Ocker Hill station after being diverted via the Princes End branch because of electrification works on the main line near Wolverhampton, 7 April 1965. The station at Ocker Hill opened in 1864 but closed in 1890 following competition from the parallel Wednesbury to Princes End tram route. It reopened in 1895 but closed in 1916 as a wartime economy measure and never reopened. The large pipe across the railway is the 30 in gas main from the Mond gasworks at Dudley Port serving industrial installations in Wednesbury, Walsall, Darlaston and Willenhall.

The absence of overhead wires dates this postcard prior to the introduction of electric trams in 1907, which means that the Crown & Cushion pub was almost brand new, having been rebuilt in 1902 from an older pub that had existed from at least 1834. Apart from the loss of the right hand gable in the mid-1980s the building has survived in a fairly complete and original condition, a rarity in these days of widespread vandalism by brewery companies. To the left stands the small printing establishment of Josiah W. Gittins, converted in more recent times into a newsagent's shop which survived until 1997.

Dickenson Brothers of Ocker Hill published several postcard views of the locality in the decade up to the First World War including this view across the tramlines in Gospel Oak Road from outside the Crown & Cushion. The gardens are laid out over the cut-and-cover tunnel that carried the Princes End branch railway under Ocker Hill island and belonged to the imposing house at 102 Ocker Hill Road, occupied by Dr A.S. Neilson in the 1950s–60s. The spire beyond the house belonged to the Ocker Hill Methodist Sunday school.

The interior of St Mark's church, Ocker Hill, consecrated on 13 November 1849. The style of the church is Decorated Gothic built with hard Staffordshire blue bricks with plentiful stone dressings at a cost of about £2,500 raised by grants and subscriptions. Plans to build a tower and spire were thwarted by mining operations, which gave rise to severe subsidence problems in the structure.

Four of the key figures in the life of St Mark's church in the 1940s were, left to right, Mr J. Vaughan, sexton; Revd Fred Brighton, vicar 1942–6 and author of *Venice of the Midlands*, a history of Ocker Hill; Mr William C. Lockett, headmaster of Ocker Hill Church of England school in Spring Street and Mr Arthur Edward Bannister, church organist and former councillor (see p. 47).

The Ocker Hill Wesleyan Society was founded way back in 1813 and this chapel was constructed in 1874. A thriving Wesleyan group existed at Ocker Hill, as shown by the collections for the opening services totalling £402. Next to the church is the Three Horseshoes. A modern building on the site of a far older house, the pub was once owned by Mrs Elizabeth Harding, the great-granddaughter of the famous pugilist, the Tipton Slasher. The chapel was demolished on 19 August 1968.

The St Mark's school football team 1911–12, with Mr R.G. Turley, headmaster, on the left and Revd H.C.A. Colville, vicar from 1908 to 1917, on the right. Mr Turley later went on to become headmaster at Princes End Joint School. St Mark's was established in 1858, being one of six National Schools in Tipton provided by the Church of England for the education of the poor before the advent of state schools. It was demolished in the 1960s.

The canal workshops and pumping station at Ocker Hill became the engineering nerve centre of the Birmingham Canal Navigations (BCN) system. Situated at the end of the 1,000 yds long Ocker Hill branch, opened in 1774, they are viewed from Moat House footbridge with the new council estates encroaching on both sides, in the late 1930s. On the right are houses in Highfield Road and Beech Crescent and to the left St Mark's Road and the 'Lost City' estate, so called because it was hemmed in by railway, canal and derelict land. The top of St Mark's church is just peering over the rooftops. This length of canal disappeared with the demolition of the workshops in 1960 when the land was reclaimed for council housing.

The pumping station at Ocker Hill was established in 1784 to re-circulate water from the Walsall canal, rising 66 ft to the Birmingham level. It became the largest such plant on the BCN network. In 1903–4 new pumps were installed which consisted of three vertical triple expansion engines built by Hawthorn Devey of Leeds. The maximum capacity was 1,048 locks or 26.2m gallons per day. The engines last worked in 1948 and were scrapped in 1960 when the site was cleared for the Bolton Court multi-storey flats development.

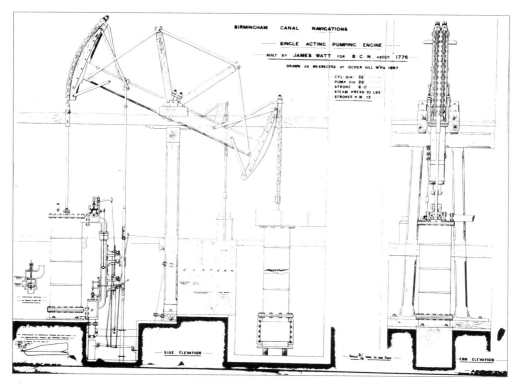

The BCN depot at Ocker Hill achieved international fame in engineering circles in 1897 when the oldest Boulton and Watt steam engine was moved from its original site in Smethwick, where it had pumped since 1779, to a specially built engine house at Ocker Hill for preservation. It was steamed for the centenary of James Watt's death in 1919 and inspected by motor car magnate Henry Ford who wanted to buy it for his museum in America, but the company refused. With the closure of the works the engine was dismantled in 1959 and transferred to the Museum of Science and Industry in Birmingham where it was restored to working order in 1983 as the world's oldest working steam engine. This 1919 drawing shows the arrangement of the engine at Ocker Hill.

The Drayton was probably Tipton's least known and shortest-lived public house. It was built in the mid-1950s at the corner of Coronation Road and Hawthorn Road on the 'Lost City' estate. The pub was demolished around 1980 when the site was redeveloped for housing. This photograph is dated 6 October 1969.

As the name implies, Moat Farm stood surrounded on three sides by a moat. Sited near Hall Lane it was the home farm of the manor, first mentioned in 1690 in the survey of Humphrey Wyrley, lord of the manor. In 1799 it was in the possession of Elizabeth Smith, widow, and the last occupant was a Mr Cliff who fought a losing battle against the encroachment of coal mines on the farm's fields. It is remembered today in the street name Moat Road.

James Callear was born at Ocker Hill in 1885 and worked in the iron trade. A typical Black Country type, politically a Liberal, his sympathies lay strongly with the working classes. For 36 years a member of the Iron and Steel Federation, he became a councillor on Tipton UDC and was a strong advocate of the provision of a public park at Ocker Hill. In 1894 he appeared before a Royal Commission dealing with the problems of the aged, and there suggested an 'old age pension' which later became a reality. His son Sgt Harry Callear, a teacher at Great Bridge Schools, was killed at the Battle of the Somme. Their name is perpetuated in Callear Road.

A sketch of Cotterill's Farm as it appeared in 1927, drawn by Mr Bert Richards. This was one of Tipton's oldest farms; the date 1538 could be seen at the base of the main chimney. When the building was demolished just before the Second World War the workmen snapped three steel hawsers while trying to dislodge the main chimneystack. Its site was used to build a housing estate and its name is perpetuated in Cotterills Road.

Tipton is nationally famous for its athletics club, the Tipton Harriers, but few people nowadays would suspect a connection with country pursuits. In ancient times however this was hunting country and, when the Harrier public house in Powis Avenue was opened in the 1950s, its sign depicted a harrier bird and a marathon runner. Its position is close to the site of the old Cotterill's Farm.

The Waggon & Horses, Toll End Road, in August 1968. It was one of three pubs with that name in Tipton, the others being in Dudley Port and Dudley Road. The rear of the building looks down on the Lower Ocker Hill branch canal, which enjoyed a renaissance in the 1990s with the development of residential mooring facilities.

Coal boats wait their turn to be unloaded at Ocker Hill Power Station, *c.* 1949. In the early 1950s the Midlands Division of the British Electricity Authority was operating 129 of its own boats, in addition to hiring from contractors, to deliver coal to its Black Country and Birmingham power stations from Sandwell Park and Jubilee collieries in West Bromwich plus various Cannock Chase pits. Canal traffic ceased in September 1960 after which all coal arrived by rail.

As befitted Tipton's position on the canal system, several boatbuilding and repair yards were established within its boundaries. No fewer than seven yards were recorded in 1888 including this example belonging to Benjamin Aston near the junction of the Walsall and Toll End Communication canals, near the end of Moors Mill Lane. The firm was later styled variously as J. & B. Aston and H. & W. Aston, its best known proprietor being Joseph Aston (1849–1925) who served on Tipton Council from 1910. Workmen pose in front of a wooden boat under repair with some of the tools of their trade in the early years of the twentieth century.

Ocker Hill Post Office at 85 Toll End Road in August 1968, before it was transferred 200 yds down the road to no. 55D in 1973. The reason for this was that 80–96 Toll End Road were acquired by the council for demolition to allow the extension of Powis Avenue through to Toll End Road at this point. The longstanding postmistress at Ocker Hill during the 1930s, '40s and '50s was Miss Hilda Lockett, the sister of Billy Lockett, headmaster of Ocker Hill Church of England school in Spring Street.

Ocker Hill developed a tradition of celebrating special events with massive bonfires on the Cupfields near what is now the junction of Cupfields Avenue and Powis Avenue. They were built by workmen from the BCN canal workshops using scrap timber from old lock gates and narrowboats. The 1911 Coronation bonfire was one of the largest ever at a height of 65 ft with an estimated 260 tons of wood and became the subject of several commercial postcards such as this one published by J.W. Bernard of Union Street, Wednesbury. The building to the immediate left of the bonfire is thought to be the Golden Cup in Toll End Road.

The date is May Day 1941 and in the yard of Humphries' dairy in Toll End Road stands one of their horse-drawn milk floats with three generations of the family. Alongside the horse is John Humphries with his son Jack Dewson on the cart holding grandson David John. On the right with the reins in his hand is employee William Boaz but the figure on the left is unidentified. The dairy operated on this site from 1933 until 1968.

Humphries' dairy phased out their six horses between 1953 and 1963 and replaced them with the same number of electric milk floats. They also ran a 15 cwt Bedford and two 3 ton Karriers; one of these is seen when new in 1964 behind the dairy in Bankfield Road. All the vehicles from the horse-drawn days were painted in a brush-grained light oak with lettering in cream with green shading.

Licensee Walter Randall stands outside The Plough, 30 Aston Street, in the early 1920s. In common with a sizeable number of pubs at the time it was licensed for beer, porter and cider only and was therefore classified as a beerhouse. Only premises with a full licence inclusive of spirits could properly be called public houses. Kelly's Directory of 1928 listed Tipton's licensed premises, comprising 65 public houses and 44 beerhouses, although this did not include The Plough which seems to have closed by that date.

The view from Bridge Road of lock no. 7 on the Toll End Communication canal on a chilly Boxing Day 1965 with Tipton cemetery on the left and houses in Cotterills Road to the right. The canal was not legally abandoned until 1966 but had been out of use for several years. In November 1962 the Inland Waterways Association as part of its crusade to save the nation's canals organised a cruise on the Toll End link but were thwarted by immovable lock gates despite the efforts of divers to remove underwater debris. Thus through the 1960s and '70s British Waterways and successive local councils by their neglect allowed this fine environmental asset to be destroyed.

The Dewdrop Inn, 33 Toll End Road, pictured when Joseph Richards held a beerhouse licence in the 1930s. The unusual name is a pun on 'do drop in' (and have a drink). The etched glass windows advertise Darby's Ales, which were brewed at the Dunkirk Brewery, Greets Green, West Bromwich. The company was taken over by Mitchell's & Butler's in 1951 and closed in 1953.

The Black Country was not just a man's world. The polishing shop at the original Triplex foundry in Toll End was completely operated by female employees in the 1920s. The ladies seem to be polishing parts for fire grates. The lack of facemasks in a polishing shop indicate that health and safety regulations were not too strict at that time.

4

Horseley Heath &
Great Bridge

William Woolley Doughty was born in 1864 at Horseley Heath, the son of William Doughty, a hinge manufacturer. He was a man of determination who took over the running of the family business and gained a seat on Tipton Board of Health in 1892. This was the beginning of a long and eventful public life. He became a member of the new Tipton Urban District Council in 1895 and served until 1928. During this time he was chairman of the council for seven terms between 1917 and 1925. In 1906 as chairman of the Libraries Committee he opened the town's first permanent free library, the Central library in Victoria Road. Often conspicuous in his bright red waistcoat, he was a member of Staffordshire County Council for some years and also served as a magistrate.

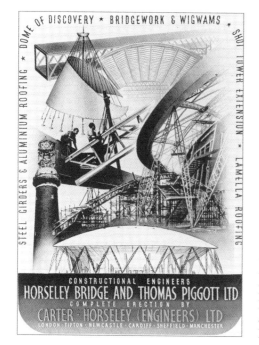

The Horseley Company was probably Tipton's most famous industrial name and certainly the longest lived. It was established as the Horseley Colliery Company in 1792 on land between the Toll End Communication canal and what is now Powis Avenue. An ironworks was built in 1809 followed by an engineering works in 1816. Technical development and achievement continued apace throughout the nineteenth and twentieth centuries, one of the highlights being the design and construction of the Dome of Discovery, centrepiece of the 1951 Festival of Britain in London. This advert, featuring the dome and other constructional elements contributed by Horseley, appeared in the Festival guidebook.

In 1865 the company moved to a new site half a mile away in Horseley Road, seen in the foreground of this aerial view from the 1950s. The works are sandwiched between Dixon's branch canal on the left and the South Staffordshire railway line on the right, from which a connection to the works sidings was obtained. On the far side of the railway is the pipe works developed in the mid-1930s after the merger with Thomas Piggott. A section of the pipe works roof still has its wartime camouflage. Great Bridge can be seen in the distance.

During the Second World War the company, in common with most industries, received government orders for the war effort. These included shell plating for ships, armoured tank bodies, bombs, mines, pontoons and sections of tank landing craft such as this example recorded in 1942 with the workmen responsible. Typical of the period, the work force is mainly middle aged and elderly. More than 270 Horseley men served in the armed forces during 1939–45, ten of them making the ultimate sacrifice.

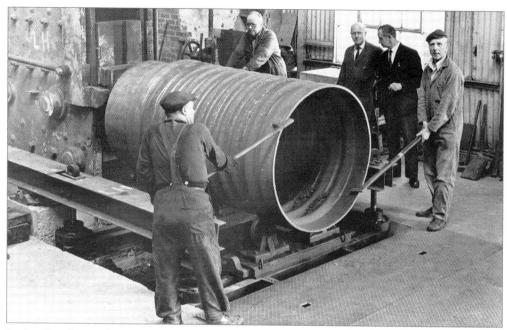

In the Horseley works press shop a section of ship's furnace flue is being passed through a power press to form corrugations and thus increase its surface area, *c*. 1970. The two men in suits looking on are Frank Grainger (left), the press shop foreman, and Will Follows, the works superintendent. Following a series of mergers between 1969 and 1989 the Horseley works closed in May 1992, the year in which the company should have been celebrating a glorious 200th anniversary.

In 1928 the Horseley Company merged with Thomas Piggott of Birmingham and adopted the new title of Horseley Bridge and Thomas Piggott, or Horseley Piggott for short, although Tipton people continued to refer to the firm simply as 'Th 'Ossley'. Piggotts had specialised in the construction of gasholders and large steel pipes and this work was eventually transferred to the Tipton site. A further type of work to develop in the postwar era was the manufacture of pressure vessels and one such is here awaiting dispatch from the works on a Scammell lorry in the early 1950s.

Tipton's General Post Office at Horseley Heath, *c.* 1909. The building with the wonderful terracotta crown above its main doorway was constructed around 1900, superseding the existing office, which stood at Dudley Port near Lower Church Lane. Note the postal workers, one with bicycle, posing near the side entrance. The office hours as advertised in those early days were 6.30am until 10pm.

William John Hayward and Company was established in 1852 and became proprietors of the Horseley Collieries which were located just to the north of the Horseley Engineering Works. By the 1930s the firm described itself as 'colliery proprietors, coal, coke and foundry coke merchants' and offered deliveries by boat, wagon, lorry or barrow. Here one of their boats, probably on the Cannock extension canal, is collecting coal to bring back to their wharf on the Dixon's branch in Horseley Heath.

Three regulars at the Prince Regent pub, Horsele
Heath, admire the stuffed ape, which once
belonged to the prizefighter, the Tipton Slasher. T
story goes that the ape was killed by the Slasher'
father who knocked it down a flight of stairs afte
being bitten on the finger. So distressed was the
Slasher that he had it stuffed. It was passed on to
his great-granddaughter Mrs Elizabeth Harding
the Three Horse Shoes in Ocker Hill who gave it
the licensee of the Horseley Heath pub when she
retired in 1940. A portrait of the Slasher also in
Mrs Harding's possession eventually found its wa
to Tipton Library, thanks to Mr J.C. Fisher of Parl
Lane East. It is believed that the ape was
ceremoniously burnt at the rear of the pub in the
early 1960s.

typical Black Country street corner pub, the White Rose, an Ansell's house standing at the junction of Horseley ath and Ballfields, August 1968. It was demolished in 1972 along with many of the mid-nineteenth-century operties that lined the main road between Great Bridge and Dudley Port.

posite: Jack Davis's milk float, powered by the 29-year-old Dinah, holds up the traffic in Horseley Heath as they ake their way back towards Great Bridge, March 1966. Jack ran his one-man milk delivery service from hitehall Road, Greets Green, relying solely on horsepower until 1968 when the death of one of his horses forced m to acquire a motorised van. He then had to employ a driver, as he did not hold a licence himself. However nah carried on with deliveries for two days a week until her death in 1971, making Jack Davis the Black untry's last horse-powered milkman.

This elevated viewpoint gives a good impression of the layout of Great Bridge market being held on its constricted triangular pitch in front of the Limerick on 22 September 1971. This 150-year-old market was relocated to a site at the corner of Mill Street a short distance away but was not a success. Despite constant appeals from the local community it never returned to its original site.

The attractive façade of the Nag's Head Inn at the corner of Market Place and Mill Street, 1962. It was built just before the First World War by Holder's Brewery of Birmingham, whose name was displayed in the etched glass front windows until their unfortunate replacement around 1990. As the Headquarters of the Tipton British Legion, the Nag's Head was chosen by Tipton Civic Society as the site for its plaque commemorating Joseph Davies VC, the only Tipton-born holder of that award. In 1998, in further recognition of Davies, who had served in the Royal Welch Fusiliers, the pub was renamed The Fusilier.

A no. 3 bus service turns out of Market Street at the start of its journey to Yew Tree Estate via West Bromwich on a snowy New Year's Day in 1977. Saxon's on the right was a highly regarded, long established fancy goods shop, which had just closed down. The buildings were eventually demolished in the late 1980s to make way for a traffic island, the first phase of the Black Country new road, which allowed through traffic to bypass Great Bridge.

A former West Bromwich Corporation bus in the drab colours of the WMPTE has just departed the Market Street terminus and is about to cross the old Tipton Borough boundary into the West Bromwich side of Great Bridge with a no. 3 service to Yew Tree Estate, Walsall, 4 April 1975. Just behind the bus is the bridge over the Haines branch canal which still displays the diamond-shaped canal company sign stating the maximum vehicle axle loads allowed.

The last place in Tipton where a colourful array of traditional working narrowboats could be seen was on t
Haines branch canal in Great Bridge, where the timber yard of Tailby and Cox took delivery of imported timb
carried from Brentford via the Grand Union Canal. The traffic lasted until 1966 and Tailby and Cox themselv
had ceased to trade by 1970.

Opposite: Characteristic features of the Black Country canal system were the interchange basins where goods we
transferred from boat to rail and vice versa. Tipton had five of these, including this one at the bottom of Ryde
Green locks in Great Bridge, built in the 1850s by the London and North Western Railway. Although interchan
use ceased in the 1940s, by the time of this 1968 picture the rail sidings were still active as part of the British Ra
steel terminal. In the basin sits a Caggy Stevens 'joey boat' which, judging by the reed growth on board, seems
have been long abandoned.

...me Road looking west from the Haines branch canal bridge in March 1966 before the houses on each side of ...e junction with Lewis Street were demolished around 1970. The Seven Stars pub, a 1920s rebuild of an older ...erhouse, was renamed the Tame Bridge in 1990 after the adjacent River Tame, which formed the old borough ...undary between Tipton and West Bromwich.

The West Bromwich Corporation circular bus route no. 28 was re-numbered 40 by the WMPTE. Seen here is one of the reduced height buses designed to pass beneath the aqueduct in Hydes Road, Wednesbury, 30 May 1975. The vehicle is passing from Bagnall Street, West Bromwich, into Eagle Lane across the old borough boundary marked by the course of the River Tame, which flowed beneath the road at this point. In the background is part of the extensive non-ferrous metal works of Ratcliff's (Great Bridge) Limited which closed down over Christmas 1989.

The original Tipton Tavern with its distinctive high steps, sketched by Bert Richards in 1937, had existed since the 1820s. In the early hours of Saturday 17 May 1941 it was destroyed by an enemy bomb, which also demolished the adjacent New Road Methodist chapel and Dr Hamilton's surgery, killing the doctor and his wife. A second bomb landed at the junction of Horseley Road and Bridge Road, severing gas and water mains. The total death toll was six with many seriously injured. After the war a new pub was built on the site, which in 1996 changed its name to the Hallbridge Arms.

e Rising Sun, seen in June 1969,
a late Victorian rebuild of a pub
iich had existed since the 1860s.
spite ruthless modernisation in
e early 1980s which destroyed
ich of the original bar fittings
d joinery the pub achieved
ebrity status in 1999 when the
mpaign for Real Ale declared it
e winner of their national Pub of
e Year award. Licensees Penny
cDonald and Jackie Walker then
ent on to be runners-up in Tipton
vic Society's Tiptonian of the Year
mpetition for their charity
indraising work.

The entrance to Tipton cemetery *c.* 1900 in Alexandra Road (formerly Workhouse Lane), which opened
in 1872. The gothic spire is the centrepiece of the two chapels, Church of England on one side and
Nonconformist on the other. In the cemetery are the graves of old Tipton residents, some covered by
ostentatious monuments and headstones. Among these are the former chairman of the Tipton School
board, William Bedworth; one-time chairman of the Tipton Urban District Council, George S. Peake;
former local Board of Health member, Thomas Downes and medical officer William Lees Underhill.

The Shrubbery public house shortly after it opened on 10 March 1939. The landlord was Jack Summerton, who had previously kept the Turf Tavern in Aston Street. The Shrubbery took its name from the tree-lined approaches and gardens to Horseley House, where Clarkes Grove now stands. The house was occupied in the final years of the eighteenth century by Joseph Amphlett, one of the original partners of the Horseley Company. The name Amphlett and several others connected to the history of the Horseley Ironworks are perpetuated in the new street names that now cover the site of the former works.

Tipton Central Schools were opened by Councillor Simeon Webb JP on 13 October 1927 and divided into separate sections for boys and girls. After the Second World War the school achieved a new status as Tipton Grammar School and in 1954 the two sections were amalgamated. The staff of the newly mixed school pose for an official photograph in one of the quadrangles with the headmaster Mr G.S. Smith seated fifth from the left on the front row.

The absence of cars, stone pavement details and gas lamp contribute a period atmosphere to this picture of St Martin's church and Tipton police station in 1953. The Georgian church tower, completed in 1797 and topped with a masonry dome complete with a ball and weathervane, was one of Tipton's most distinctive architectural features and earned the parish church the local soubriquet of 'the pepperbox'.

Revd A.W.C. Thomas looks on as workmen demolish the dome in preparation for the rebuilding of the tower, June 1963. It was never to be fully completed. This was a tragic loss, particularly as the tower represented the public consciousness of the parish church through its affectionate nickname. In remembrance of the tower one of the 1990s new roads on the adjacent gasworks site was named Pepperbox Close.

Anatomy of change: this and the next three pictures. The Cottage Spring beerhouse, Workhouse Lane, is first pictured in the late nineteenth century when the landlord was John Whitehouse Jevons, whose licence allowed him also to brew beer on the premises. The pub is obviously a combination of two cottages, the left hand door having been bricked up and the right hand opening, with its wooden door case, brought into use as the main entrance.

Workhouse Lane was renamed Alexandra Road during the reign of Edward VII in honour of Queen Alexandra. During the 1910s and '20s Mrs Phoebe Gould held the licence of the Cottage Spring and this was passed to Sidney J. Gould, presumably her son, in the 1930s, by which time this grand three-storey brewery had been built. Note also the change made in the first floor windows where the eight pane sashes have been placed by a two pane pattern.

The Flying Standard car means that this picture was taken no earlier than 1936 and, as Sidney Gould no longer held the licence of the Cottage Spring by 1940, it can be dated between those years. A further passage of time has seen the brickwork rendered and the sashes of the bay replaced by more utilitarian fixed panes with top lights. These alterations, together with the removal of the door case and the replacement of the bull-nosed stone steps with concrete, have begun to erode the original character of the pub.

After the Second World War the pub was acquired by Banks's and the brewery building demolished, ironically to make way for a new toilet block. A further modification was the replacement of the original left hand bar window with a wider steel-framed opening typical of the 1950s. Despite these alterations this 1968 view shows that the signboard has survived three-quarters of a century with just an occasional repaint to reflect the changing ownership. The Cottage Spring was extensively refurbished in the 1980s but is still recognisable as the building in the earliest picture.

The Furnace Inn, Howard Street, had closed and reverted to use as an ordinary house by the time of this August 1968 picture but it still carried an advert for Ansell's beers. It may well have derived its name from the iron founding company owned by Joseph Onions, which stood around the corner in Keelinge Street in the late nineteenth century. A substantial building, its unusual arched window above the entrance suggests that it once had another use, maybe as the iron foundry manager's house.

The first ever royal visit to Tipton was when Princess Marie Louise of Schleswig-Holstein came to open the Staffordshire Home for Nurses in Lower Church Lane on 3 August 1909 (see also p. 13). The movement for supplying trained nurses had begun with the formation of the Ocker Hill Nurses' Association in 1907 and the formation of the Tipton Nursing Association the following year. The Princess took a keen interest in the work of nurses and did much to further their pursuits.

One of Tipton's traditional industries to survive into the twenty-first century is the Dudley Port Rolling Mills, located on the bank of Dixon's branch canal in Lower Church Lane. A group of workers take a break from their labours for an official photograph, 1929.

Martha Powell, wife of prominent councillor Joseph Powell, was born in 1856. Not a suffragette but a keen advocate of 'Votes for Women' she supported any efforts to improve women's role in public life. When young she had a scholastic training and eventually became headmistress of Dudley Port Girls' School, a post she resigned on marriage. She then became involved in numerous good causes including the British Women's Temperance Association of which she was a member of the national executive. Always interested in the less advantaged, in 1898 she was publicly elected as a Guardian of the Poor for Tipton, an office she held for some time. She was a prolific writer on such subjects as the Poor Law, the working classes, hygiene, cookery and Black Country life, and also a clear and precise public speaker. Powell Place recalls the public life of this husband and wife partnership.

Tipton gained its own version of the Blackpool illuminations in the late 1960s when the towering structures of the new gasworks were lit up for the night. The new gasworks went into production in 1965. Its high pressure reforming plants were originally designed to use naphtha but were later modified to convert natural gas into manufactured gas. At its peak Tipton was capable of producing 300m cu ft of gas per day. The conversion of appliances to natural gas led to its decline and production ceased in March 1975.

A mid-1970s aerial view of the new Tipton gasworks, reputedly the largest plant of its kind in Europe. This was surrounded by a variety of housing styles, from the Edwardian Park Estate known as The Terraces, the 1930s council houses in Anderson Road, the 1930s private houses in Victoria Road and, in the distance, the 1960s multi-storey flats of St Martin's House. The gasworks site was redeveloped as a private housing estate in the 1990s.

Pub checks from the Great Bridge and Horseley Heath areas. The Rising Sun, Horseley Road, still open (see p. 77); Railway Inn, New Road, closed *c.* 1980; Nag's Head, corner of Mill Street, still open (see p. 72); The Stork, on the West Bromwich side of Great Bridge, closed 1985; Seven Stars, Tame Road, still open (see p. 75); Horseley Tavern, Horseley Heath, still open; Star Inn, corner of Tame Road, still open and the Vine Inn, the other corner of Tame Road opposite The Star, closed late 1930s.

Tucked in among the mid-nineteenth-century houses of the lower part of Lower Church Lane was the Swan off-licence, pictured around 1969 a few years before its demolition. The door and window details are of architectural interest.

William Purchase and his wife stand outside their shop at 87 Lower Church Lane, *c.* 1920. From the window display it appears that their main business was confectionery but the sign over the door reveals that Purchase is also licensed to sell tobacco. The building, which survived until the 1960s, was located on the Horseley Heath side of the bridge that carried Lower Church Lane over the Dudley to Walsall railway line.

A group of young children from Lower Church Lane and Horseley Heath perform a pageant to help raise money towards the war effort in 1916. The children are patriotically dressed, some as nurses and some as wounded soldiers. The little girl with the cross on her uniform is Amy Cliff of Lower Church Lane.

5

Burnt Tree, Dudley Port & Tividale

George Samuel Peake was born in Nottingham in 1845 and moved to Darlaston at an early age, then on to Tipton where he was later to set up business as a pawnbroker at Dudley Port in premises near the station. In 1878 he filled a vacancy on the Tipton local Board of Health and in 1895 when Tipton UDC was set up he became one of its original members. He represented Horseley Heath and Dudley Port wards at various times and was chairman of the council in 1913, 1915 and 1916. In 1907 he became chairman of the Dudley Board of Guardians. During his long life he was involved with Tipton's local government for 50 years. He died in 1926 and is buried with his family in Tipton cemetery. His name is perpetuated in Peake Drive, near to where he lived in Dudley Port.

The wall calendars reveal that the year is 1933 in Class 4 of Dudley Port infants' school and, inevitably, two of the children cannot remain still long enough for the duration of the camera's time exposure. The school was built in 1875 by the Tipton School Board for a capacity of 500 juniors and 250 infants and was situated adjacent to Dudley Port station on land now occupied by Smith Place. The schools closed in 1938 but the buildings were not demolished until 1954.

The Royal Oak near Dudley Port railway station has been a popular hostelry for many years. In 1854 the public enquiry for the granting of local Board of Health status was held there, paving the way for local government in Tipton in its modern form. In more recent years Tipton Civic Society has held its meetings there. In this view of the pub in 1963, a Hurley's bread van is making deliveries.

n atmospheric night-time shot of Dudley Port as passengers board a Birmingham Corporation no. 74 bus for udley while a train pauses at the High Level station on the bridge above in 1953. This scene changed forever in 964 when the blue brick railway arch was blown up in preparation for the rebuilding of the station and ectrification of the line. The smaller span of the Ryland canal aqueduct beyond was rebuilt in 1967.

Above: Surveyors examine blast furnace slag just south of Dudley Port station, mid-1950s. The site was to be reclaimed for the Vono sports ground that was eventually to open in July 1957. As well as clearing away slag the work also involved culverting the Groveland brook. The early nineteenth-century houses in the background on the west side of the main road were soon to be demolished to make way for blocks of council flats.

Left: Holcroft's Portfield Iron & Galvanising Works was established on the bank of the Old Main Line canal at Dudley Port in the 1860s and worked until the 1920s when this rare photograph records one of their stacks being dropped on 5 June 1925 following closure of the works. Their memory is perpetuated by the nearby Holcroft Street and Portfield Drive. The disused pithead gear is a reminder of Tipton's other great industry, coal mining, which, following a long decline from the late nineteenth century, had become extinct by the 1920s.

The Hop & Barleycorn public house in Dudley Port dated from the mid-nineteenth century. Thomas Roberts was the owner in 1851; one John Pessol was licensee in 1865. A typical Black Country pub with two bay windows flanking a central doorway, it lasted until well past the Second World War when its external wall had become deformed by mining subsidence. The room on the right was the taproom; the frosted window advertises Holder's beer.

Mary Jane Preece stands with some of her family outside her shop at 127 Dudley Port, midway between the Old Port Hotel and Tividale Street. The shop is decorated with bunting thought to be in celebration of the end of the First World War in 1918. The poster on the right is advertising the film *Woman in Black* showing at the Tivoli cinema (which was later to become the Regent) in Owen Street.

Samuel Wilkes, who lived at Dudley Port, became the self-styled 'Champion Woodcarver of England' when at the turn of the nineteenth century he carved a chain from a plank of wood. This chain was 82 ft long, and had 472 links, two hooks and a swivel (now in Birmingham Museum). He also carved many other models. Here Samuel is seen with members of his family, c. 1930. Back row: (children) Lydia, Ted, Tom, Fanny. Front row: Samuel, Rose (daughter-in-law), Jessie (granddaughter), a friend, Charlotte (wife). Charlotte, known locally as Granny Wilkes, was noted for her herbal remedies.

Tividale Street Primitive Methodist chapel stood at the corner of Dudley Port and Tividale Street from 1905 to 1990, its last service being held on 3 November. The new Dudley Port Methodist Centre was built on the site, and held its inaugural service almost exactly one year later on 9 November 1991. This 1965 picture gives a view of Tividale Street and Hadley's painters and decorators shop on the opposite corner to the chapel.

...ornington House, Dudley Port, ...e home of John Freakley ...842–1911), who was well ...own in Tipton as a slag ...ntractor. The house was quite ...and, standing out from its ...ighbours because of its ornate ...eze and finials and fine tall ...imneys. The sign states ...ontractors for the supply of ...ast Furnace Slag' and John ...eakley and Company Limited ...ntinued to operate from here ...til the 1960s. A similar house ...xt door contained Burnt Tree ...st Office.

A view of S.F. Riley's car showroom situated just below the junction of Coneygre Road where Dudley Port gives way to Burnt Tree, 1965. Syd Riley began his business a few years after the Second World War, selling the odd car outside a private house further down the road. He then moved to these premises formerly owned by the haulage contractor E.J. Howell, before moving on to an even bigger site just below Tividale Street.

...1967 the Roman Mosaic ...mpany Ltd of Burnt Tree ...veiled this magnificent mural, ...easuring 100 ft by 20 ft, made ...m 1.5 million cubes of vitreous ...ass. Appropriately its theme was ...man architecture and the artist ...s Mr E. De Rosa, a director of ...e company, seen here with his ...ation. The firm vacated the site ...1987 and the mosaic was ...corporated into the façade of a ...w pub, Sawyers, which in 1999 ...s transformed into a restaurant ...h the unfortunate result of ...mpletely obliterating this ...usual work of art.

A postcard view of Tividale Road c. 1905, showing the brand new electric tramway and well-appointe villas which ensured that this top e of Tividale was a desirable residenti area in the early decades of the twentieth century. The Birminghan to Dudley tram route had been operated by steam trams from 188 and electrified in 1904. It became t last section of tramway to operate i the Black Country, closing on 30 September 1939.

St Michael's church was built in 1877–8 at a cost of £11,390 with seating for 750 worshippers. Its tower dominated the district and when new looked down on the activities of Tividale Hall and Burnt Tree collieries, then later on the tram workshops where Black Country tramcars were built and repaired.

The interior of St Michael's church showing the large crucifix mounte above the chancel screen. In 1982 the building was found to be riddle with wet and dry rot, which requir an estimated £75,000 to rectify. T Church Council voted 15 to 10 in favour of demolition, a shock decision that devastated the congregation. The demolition took place in 1984 and a much smaller church was built on the site.

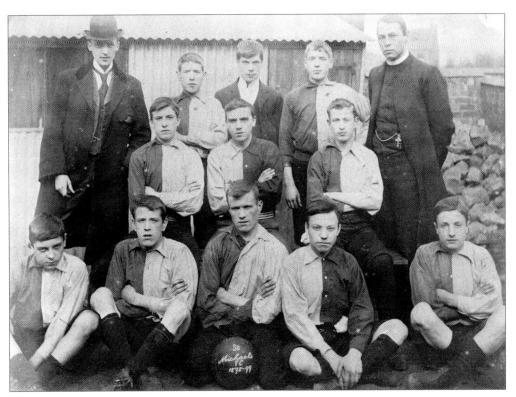

Association football was alive and thriving in the late nineteenth century, especially among the churches and chapels of the area. Here is the St Michael's church football club team for the 1898–9 season with the vicar, Revd S.G.W. Maitland.

This view looking east along Tividale Road from its junction with Hopkins Street in 1965 shows the houses that were demolished in the late 1970s, leaving the Plough as the only surviving building. The site was redeveloped in the early 1980s for council housing with a space left for a shoppers' car park next to the pub. The white building on the extreme right is the Gate Hangs Well.

From the Gate Hangs Well, the Tipton Borough boundary ran along the footpath on the left up to the last house in view, the area beyond on the right being part of the Borough of Rowley Regis. The parked Ford Anglia on the right pinpoints the former entrance to the Tividale tram workshops, which operated between 1907 and 1930. All the buildings in this 1965 scene had been demolished by the end of the 1970s.

Standing at the corner of Sedgley Road East and Cleton Street was the Groveland Brook Inn, better known simply as the 'Brook', which took its name from the adjacent watercourse. This formed the borough boundary between Tipton and Rowley Regis and the Tipton Borough sign can be seen to the left of the building. Characterised by steep steps leading up to its front door, the pub operated on a six-day licence. When photographed in the mid-1950s it had closed down but it later reopened for a few years as a sports club.

ub checks from the Burnt
ree, Dudley Port and
vidale areas. Jolly Brewer
n, near the corner of
rnt Tree and Bradley
reet, closed 1980;
aggon & Horses Inn on
e corner of Dudley Road
d Groveland Road just
tside Tipton Borough,
ll open after rebuilding in
e late 1970s; Brown Lion
n, corner of Coneygre
ad and Tudor Street,
osed c. 1937 (see p. 106);
iners Arms, location
nknown; Wellington Inn,
rk Lane East, closed
999.

he Vono Company, whose name was an acronym of 'Vaughan Only No Other' after its founder, Mr Vaughan,
arted in 1896 as general ironfounders in Groveland Road. Moving to a larger site in Sedgley Road East they
eveloped into bed and mattress manufacture and by the 1950s claimed to possess the largest single
anufacturing unit of bedding and upholstery in the UK. This 1928 picture shows part of their extensive
oodworking shop.

Vono's dark blue Thames Trader delivery vans were a familiar sight in the 1950s and '60s and this line-up in front of the factory around 1960 illustrates the scale of operations. In 1958 the firm was proud that it was the only British furniture company to exhibit at the Brussels Universal and International Exhibition. Also displaying its products in the British Industry pavilion at the time was the neighbouring Revo Electric Company.

A West Bromwich Corporation Transport no. 74 double decker bus mounts the humpbacked bridge over the Old Main Line canal at Dudley Port in 1958. It approaches the Old Port Hotel, which took its name from the original Dudley Port, having just passed the Bell public house further down the road. The bridge was rebuilt and widened in 1963 as the first phase of what was to be a dual carriageway from Great Bridge to Burnt Tree Island. On completion it was criticised as still having too much of a hump.

The new bridge viewed from the canal in June 1969, by which time the Old Port Hotel had closed and been converted to a garage. Note the narrowboat graveyard on the right, a familiar sight on Black Country canals in the 1960s following the end of commercial carrying, all a far cry from the late eighteenth and early nineteenth centuries when the spot was the port for Dudley, where goods for that town were loaded and unloaded. This was of course the origin of the name Dudley Port.

Just to the west of Dudley Port on the Old Main Line canal, Coneygre Foundry was built on the site where one of the Black Country's earliest blast furnaces was operating in about 1625. Following the construction of the canal an ironworks was established in the 1790s by Zachariah Parkes. Iron making ceased in 1896, after which foundry operations continued until the 1980s with castings for the motor industry being the principal product in modern times. Following the demolition of the foundry the site was developed for housing. On the right of the picture is the attractive open space of the Coneygre sports ground laid out by Palethorpe's Ltd in the 1920s.

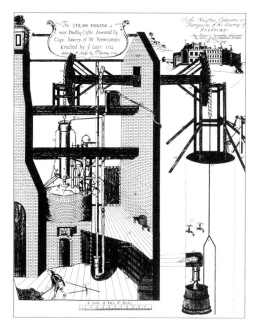

Near the spot where the railway crosses the Old Main Line canal, in 1712 there occurred an event which changed the world. Paving the way for the industrial revolution, in that year the engineer Thomas Newcomen erected the world's first successful steam engine to pump water from the Coneygre coalworks. It became known as the Dudley Castle engine owing to its proximity across open countryside to that local landmark, which can be seen in this contemporary engraving. This picture provided evidence for the construction of a full sized replica of the engine at the Black Country Museum in 1986. The achievement has also been commemorated by Tipton Civic Society in the form of a plaque on the nearby Coneygre Community Centre and in the naming of new streets on the Coneygre Foundry site as Newcomen, Calley (Newcomen's assistant) and Barney (the engraver of the illustration).

In 1862 the South Staffordshire Waterworks Company paid the earl of Dudley £3,250 for a plot of land bounded by the Old Main Line canal, the South Staffordshire Railway and Park Lane West on which to construct its Coneygre reservoir and pumping station. Two steam pumping engines supplied by Jonah and George Davis of Tipton were installed in 1864. One was replaced in 1906 by this horizontal rotative engine from James Watt and Co., and the second in 1919 by an electric pumping plant, a part of which is visible on the right.

n Edwardian view of Victoria Road and Tipton's brand new central library, which had been opened in 1906. The e gas lamps of the Tipton Gas Department lit up this smart residential road in which lived the likes of Richard ason, the Toll End brickworks owner and, at no. 22 on the extreme left, Alfred Chatwin of Sunbeam Grates fame.

e view from the entrance to South Staffordshire Waterworks depot into Park Lane West in May 1925 shows the ack Horse, Brewery Street, and the small shop belonging to Eli Scriven which in more recent times was owned Mrs Corns, a Belgian lady. All these buildings were swept away in the early 1970s.

At the rear of Mr Chatwin's house in 1940 are guests at a garden party organised by St Paul's Methodist church at Dudley Port. Mr Chatwin himself is standing fourth from the left next to his wife, while on the extreme right is the minister, Revd J.W. Jordan, and on the end of the back row Mr F. Raybould, the church organist. In the background are the Anderson Road council houses.

The central library, looking resplendent in its brick and (very) yellow terracotta work with its asymmetrically placed tower to the design of Tipton architect, George H. Wenyon, in 1955. The noticeboard advertises the Tipton Horse Show and Gymkhana, which was to be held on Victoria Park on 16 July that year. The library was transferred to a new building in the Unity Walk development off Owen Street in 2000. Despite categorical assurances from Sandwell MBC that the old building would be reoccupied by staff from another council department, it was left empty and Tipton's greatest architectural treasure now faces an uncertain future.

The Tipton librarian from 1964 to 1973 was Miss Megan Joy Higgs, seen here in 1972 with the contents of a time capsule recovered from beneath the foundation stone of the old Public Offices in Owen Street on their demolition. The stone had been laid on 15 December 1876 by James Whitehouse, chairman of the local Board of Health. The capsule contained a scroll, local newspapers and visiting cards, showing that this is not such a new idea after all.

The Park Inn on the corner of Victoria Road and Park Lane East, seen in February 1968, was built as a hotel around 1900 to replace the old Seven Stars Inn on the opposite corner, where the library now stands. It was reputedly haunted by the ghost of a little girl, who died after being accidentally trapped in an attic room. Pub landlords down the years have reported unexplained footsteps, knockings and lights being mysteriously turned on and off. The Park closed in 1996 and the building was converted to flats.

Opposite the Park Inn stood the corner grocery shop of Holloway and Son pictured with Ted Holloway on the left and his father Joseph standing with hands behind his back, late 1930s. The other two gents, friends or customers, have not been identified. The shop still bears the name of previous proprietor John Briscoe Jordan, who ran the business before the First World War. Following Holloway's departure in the mid-1950s the shop continued for 20 years in the hands of George and Margaret Jones.

A row of nineteenth-century houses standing in Sedgley Road East in the 1920s. In the centre next to the entry is a typical front room shop, simply converted from the front room of the house. Such shops often sold a wide variety of goods. On the wall near the door is a poster advertising the latest films at the Regent cinema in Owen Street. This row was demolished in the late 1930s.

At the corner of Coneygre Road and Tudor Street was the Brown Lion public house whose sign declared that fine home brewed ales could be purchased from the licensee, Annie Morris. Thought to have been built around 1850 the pub and its wonderful painted sign of a rampant lion was demolished in 1936. Near to the pub a small cottage was requisitioned in 1863 to hold Methodist New Connexion services, which eventually led to the formation of the Park Methodist Church in 1903.

he girls of the Park Methodist hurch Sunday School march along oneygre Road in the annual nniversary procession, sometime in e 1920s, watched by parents and embers of the chapel congregation nd photographed from the bedroom indow of one of the houses next to e Brown Lion. On the other side of e road is Moores field with its brick ome-covered pit shafts, a still visible gacy of Tipton's coal mining dustry.

The same anniversary parade accompanied by a local marching band. In the background can be seen the railway line. The sheds on Moores field seem to have been used as stables. The Park Methodist church was built in 1903 at a cost of £600 as a schoolroom for a church that was never built owing to lack of funds. Thus the schoolroom served as both church and Sunday school.

ipton and District Christian ndeavour Union was formed in May 920 to encourage and train young 1ethodists for positions in their espective churches. The Park 1ethodist Junior Christian ndeavourers won the Federation 1nior Challenge Banner for two uccessive years in 1935 and 1936. lere the members are seen sitting utside the chapel displaying the anner after their second chievement in 1936. The entleman standing next to the roup is Ernie Tibbetts.

Robert Raikes of Gloucester founded the Sunday School movement in 1780 giving rise to the most important event in a church or chapel's calendar, the Sunday School anniversary. These are the children of the Park Methodist church, affectionately known as the Little Chapel in Binfield Street, sitting on the platform, the girls in their white frocks and sashes, the boys in their best clothes, ready to participate in the anniversary service sometime in the 1950s.

The children of the Park Methodist church assemble in Victoria Road in July 1952 to partake in their annual Sunday school anniversary parade around the local streets, being addressed by the Revd G.A. Parrot, who led the procession. This section of the street from the Park Hotel to the railway bridge was, until 1903, a part of Coneygre Road. In that year the Park Methodists applied to Tipton UDC to change the name to Victoria Road in order to reinforce their Victoria Park identity. This was duly granted.

...nfield Street was built in the first ...ecade of the twentieth century as an ...xtension to the new Park Housing ...state constructed by William Henry ...nderson of the Midland Building ...ompany. The photographer has ...rived on a dustbin collection day in ...ly 1971 to record the 18 houses ...ith their alternating pairs of bay ...indows and the former transport ...pot of Palethorpe's Ltd at the top of ...e street. The row was demolished ...1976.

The Wellington Inn, Park Lane East, pictured in 1968, was first recorded in 1851. It may well have been opened to serve the adjacent ironworks established by Thomas Morris in 1847, which worked until about 1880 although the style of the building suggests a slightly earlier date. It was doubtless named after the Duke of Wellington (1769–1852), one of Britain's greatest military heroes, though less successful as Prime Minister from 1828 to 1830.

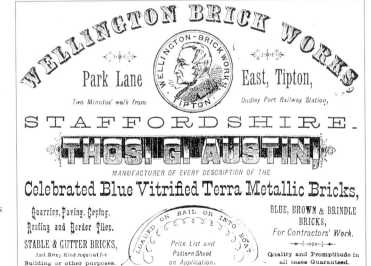

...he Wellington brickworks of Thomas G. ...ustin was situated between Park Lane ...ast and the railway embankment on ...and that was later to be occupied by ...eel Street. This 1880s advert, with its ...se of the Duke of Wellington's profile, ...dds weight to the theory that the ...djacent Wellington Inn was indeed ...amed after the Duke. Blue coping bricks ...tamped with Austin's name could be ...een in the boundary wall of the old ...ipton Green schools in Sedgley Road ...Vest, built in 1878.

Peel Street, together with Barnett and Perry Streets, was laid out in about 1900 on the site of the Wellington brickworks. The foreground of this 1968 picture was the location of the brickworks marl-pit which must have been well filled in as these terraced houses stood solidly until their demolition in 1995, although the 1920s council houses on the right did suffer from subsidence leading to their premature clearance. The street name may well be a further subtle reference to Wellington as Sir Robert Peel (1780–1850) was a political contemporary and colleague of the Iron Duke.

The well-turned-out white horses and immaculately clean wagon suggests that this is a publicity photograph for coal merchants Worthington and Pugh, of Park Lane East. Some small lettering on the wagon informs us that it was built in Tipton but the maker's name is concealed. Unfortunately, the location of this picture has not been identified.

6

Bloomfield, Princes End & Tibbington

A hard-working and dignified character, Thomas Chalstrey, born at Summerhill, was the son of the underground mine manager at a local colliery. He went into the mines at the age of thirteen but in 1894 he became an agent for the Refuge Assurance Co. His success in this department saw him rise up the ladder until in 1904 he became District Superintendent for Tipton, Wednesbury and Darlaston. In 1910 he gained a seat on Tipton Urban District Council, which he held for several years. Two generations later, in 1995–6, Thomas Chalstrey's grandson, Alderman Sir John Chalstrey, became the Lord Mayor of London, the first surgeon ever to hold that office.

The Chain, Cable and Anchor Act of 1864 made chain testing a legal requirement and led to the setting up of proving houses in the chain-producing areas including Tipton, which had developed a significant chain and anchor trade from the 1850s. Lloyd's British Testing Co. had established their proving house in a former railway goods shed at Factory Basin, Bloomfield, by 1880 and it operated until the decline of the industry in the 1930s. Seen here in a deteriorating condition in the late 1960s, Lloyd's Proving House survived long enough to become a listed building but in 1975 was half demolished by thieves removing the structural ironwork. Shortly afterwards permission was given for its complete removal.

Nos 4 to 7 Bloomfield Road were awaiting demolition when photographed from Brook Street in October 1968. The bridge carrying the Stour Valley railway had recently been rebuilt as part of the upgrading of the line for electrification and the span increased to improve the road alignment. The bridge acquired some claim to fame in the 1980s when artwork in the form of a musical score was applied to the structure. The poster partially obscured by a passing car is advertising *Carry on Camping* at the Clifton cinema, Sedgley.

The elegant façade of the Star Hotel in Bloomfield Road is decorated with Union Jacks and bunting in celebration of either the 1935 Silver Jubilee of George V or the 1937 Coronation of George VI. The Star was tragically destroyed in an air raid in November 1940 in which the licensee's son was killed. A high explosive bomb buried itself in the pavement before exploding and demolishing the rear of the building, although curiously the frontage remained intact. Five customers in the bar escaped with minor injuries.

After the war the Star Hotel was rebuilt on the same site but set back in anticipation of road widening that never materialised. The picture dates from October 1968, a couple of years before the houses on the right were cleared. The Star was demolished in April 1996 and the site is now occupied by the MOST Management Training Centre.

About a hundred yards towards Princes End on the opposite side to the Star was the Black Horse, which had been licensed as a beerhouse for most of its existence. It closed in 1995 and was later converted into a café. The former pub survives today as the oldest building in the Bloomfield area. The picture is dated July 1968.

Next to the Black Horse from 1851 to the late 1970s stood Bloomfield Methodist chapel, whose football club first XI were runners-up in the West Bromwich and District League in 1954–5. Back row, left to right: Geoff Jeavons, John James, Len White, Frank Perry, Bill Whitehouse, Dennis Webb. Front row: Jack Baker, Sam Caddick, Charlie Davis (Captain), Reg Pulley, Laurie Matthews.

An aerial view of the Brymill Steelworks in 1950 when small houses still fronted Bloomfield Road and the Old Main Line canal was still navigable. Behind the works runs the Princes End branch railway and the slag dumps remaining from the old Bloomfield ironworks, which occupied the site in the nineteenth century. Beyond the railway is Tibbington Terrace with the Princes End Joint Schools and to the right the sprawling council houses of Salter, Ivy and Laburnam Roads and Central Avenue.

By 1962 Brymill had constructed new offices and laboratories and laid out a garden frontage to Bloomfield Road following the clearance of the old houses as seen on the aerial photograph. An opening ceremony attended by the mayor of Tipton, Councillor J.W. Walters, was held for the new laboratories on 27 May 1959, at which a plaque was unveiled commemorating James Watt's first commercial beam engine which had been erected nearby in 1776 to pump water from the Bloomfield colliery. The unveiling was performed by Lord Northesk of the Newcomen Society.

The King's Arms in Bloomfield Road was one of the oldest establishments in Tipton, having been recorded in Parson and Bradshaw's directory of 1818, the earliest such trade directory to include Tipton. In the doorway stands Mrs Alice Preston who held the licence from 1913 through to the 1940s. The styles of dress indicate that the picture dates from the early years of her occupancy.

By the 1960s the King's Arms had become part of the Ansell's empire and undergone some alterations to its doors and windows. The pub closed in the 1990s and stood empty until its demolition in 2000. This photograph is dated September 1968.

Up to the 1950s when redevelopment began to take its toll, most of Tipton's main roads were lined with nineteenth-century houses and shops. These examples on the corner of Bloomfield Road and Hipkins Street, recorded on 12 March 1972, were some of the last to survive in the Bloomfield area. Hipkins Street took its name from the prominent Tipton family (see pp. 25–7), which owned a candle factory near this spot.

Before the relaxation of licensing laws allowed virtually any store to sell alcohol, off-licences such as this example at 31 Regent Street in the 1930s were an institution. They took the form of small shops licensed to sell beer only for consumption off the premises, often with handpulls installed on the counter to serve draught beer to customers bringing in their own jugs and bottles to be filled.

Many pubs in the Black Country had names which reflected the industries they served and the Jolly Collier in High Street, Princes End, was a good example, especially as it had suffered from the effects of subsidence brought about by the handiwork of the colliers themselves. By March 1972 the pub had lost its neighbouring terraced houses to make way for new light engineering works and was to survive only another two or three years before being itself demolished for further industrial expansion.

The Princes End Baptist church football team for the season 1911–12 pose in front of the house of the chapel caretaker, Tom Genner. The house was situated at the rear of the chapel in Newhall Street adjacent to the Princes End branch railway line. The team played under the name Princes End Baptist Athletic.

ub checks from Bloomfield, rinces End and Tibbington reas. The Black Horse, loomfield Road, closed 1995 ee p. 114); The Bird in Hand, ibbington Terrace, a eerhouse which existed in the 860s; The Old Coach & orses, High Street, a eerhouse which existed in the 870s; The Royal Hotel, corner f Newhall Street and loomfield Road, closed 1996 nd The Talbot Inn, Bradleys ane, which still exists.

he Prince of Wales on the corner of Bloomfield Road and Bradleys Lane as it appeared in September 1968 when he attractive finger post still directed travellers to Coseley along the B4163. The pub closed in 1979, was reduced o a single storey and converted to a pork scratchings factory. Now the only surviving clue to its former existence is he blue brick plinth with one surviving cellar vent.

W.G. Allen & Sons was established around 1850 to manufacture colliers' baskets and rakes for use in the local coalmines. The business expanded into colliery tubs, mine cars and other colliery equipment together with narrow gauge rolling stock for a wide variety of industries. This display, which includes a very highly polished 2½ ton light alloy mine car, was part of the British Industries Fair at Castle Bromwich, Birmingham, in the early 1950s. At this time Allen's claimed to be 'probably the largest and oldest manufacturers of such colliery equipment in England'.

In Allen's workshops during the 1950s a newly constructed gravity tipler device with a coal tub in position is being tested prior to dispatch. The tiplers were designed to receive loaded coal tubs at the pithead and, by revolving, discharged their contents on to conveyor belts taking the coal to be sorted and graded. Allen's closed down in 1986 after 136 years of service to the mining industry.

Princes End Post Office, 79 High Street, in 1908, a year after Joseph Brain took over as sub-postmaster. Mr Brain is seen here with his wife Betty and their dog Ponto beneath a signboard which proclaims his other trades of building contractor and funeral director. He died in 1936 and was followed by his daughter Nellie who ran the Post Office until her death in 1951.

Sixty years later the façade of the building has taken on a plainer appearance and the enamelled Victorian letter box has been replaced with a standard red pillar box accompanied by a 1936 designed K6 telephone kiosk and a stamp machine. The Post Office was relocated into the new Princes End shopping precinct in the 1970s and the site redeveloped as the Aaron Manby sheltered housing scheme.

In the late nineteenth and early twentieth centuries Tipton had two notable brass bands, the Dudley Port Excelsior Band and the Princes End Temperance Priz Band, seen here around 1911. The bandsmen accompanied events in the town such as the opening of Victoria Park in 1901 and th visit of Princess Marie Louise in 1909.

The George & Dragon, pictured in 1969, is the oldest surviving pub in Princes End, dating from at least the 1830s. Its bold fascia lettering, probably dating from the same period, is particularly noteworthy. Although Princes End has always carried a Tipton postal address, the High Street actually formed the boundary between Tipton Borough on the south side and Coseley Urban District to the north. Near the junction with Upper Church Lane the boundary made a curious detour to the south thereby placing the George & Dragon in Coseley.

The boundary line continued behind the George & Dragon on towards Gospel Oak for about 100 yds before slicing through the middle of the Coach & Horses, putting the front of the pub in Coseley and the rear in Tipton. Such strange alignments in old boundaries are often explained by their following old field patterns or water courses which pre-date urban development by hundreds of years. This photograph is dated September 1968.

The *Tipton Herald* of 31 December 1960 carried the headline 'Swans must make way for new estate', referring to the fact that the disused Old Main Line canal at Upper Church Lane was to be infilled to make way for yet more council housing. Thus the swannery with its valuable amenity was swept away by unimaginative local authority planners. The bungalows in Field Road and Gospel Oak Methodist chapel form the backdrop to this image from July 1960.

William Millington provided employment for many Tipton hands in the nineteenth century at his Summerhill ironworks, which was in production from the 1820s to the 1890s. The company was noted for its superior brands of iron, particularly chain iron, rivet iron and boilerplates. The company was known worldwide for its export trade and in 1855 won the prize medal at the Paris Exhibition. An exotic memorial to the Millington family still exists in St Martin's churchyard.

A diesel multiple unit train crosses Upper Church Lane having paused at Princes End signal box to pick up the token for the single line section down to Wednesbury, 22 November 1980. The train was an enthusiasts' special organised by the Railway Correspondence and Travel Society to tour freight-only lines in the West Midlands. Since the closure of Bilston steelworks in 1979 traffic on the Princes End branch had declined to the point when the line closed completely in April 1981, thus making this special the last ever passenger train to pass through Princes End.

ummerhill chapel, situated on the corner of Upper Church Lane and Laburnum Road near to Lathe's foundry, as one of the six establishments run by the Primitive Methodists in Tipton. A small and simple building it was pened as a mission room in 1910 and served the community until its closure and demolition around 1980. The icture is dated 5 July 1969.

pposite: The Victory Inn, situated on the corner of Upper Church Lane and Salter Road and seen here on 13 July 968, was put up in the 1920s to serve the large council housing estate then being built. It changed its name to ie Brewer & Baker in the 1970s and closed in the 1980s. The site has since been redeveloped as housing.

The Moat foundry of Charles Lathe and Co. at Upper Church Lane, Summerhill, was established in 1872 and specialised in cast iron grates and kitchen ranges. By the early 1930s, they were claiming that one million of their grates and ranges had been installed in every kind of dwelling from the humble cottage to stately mansions. Despite adapting to more modern styles of fireplace over the years the firm did not survive the end of domestic solid fuel and closed in 1969. In this photograph of *c.* 1910 other typical products such as cast iron windows and ornamental gates can be seen.

This 1920s aerial view of Lathe's works is taken from a publicity postcard produced by the firm. Upper Church Lane runs from left to right and the Old Main Line canal has almost encircled the works in one of its loops, while the junction with the Ocker Hill branch canal (see p. 55) is just visible, top right. Summerhill chapel can be seen in the centre, prior to the construction of Laburnum Road.

A group of Tipton football supporters wait to board a coach in West Bromwich High Street to take them to Wembley to watch the 1954 FA Cup Final between West Bromwich Albion and Preston North End. These folks were members of the Albion Supporters Club which met at the Tibbington pub in Central Avenue and several of these were employees of Lee-Howls Ltd. The supporters returned happily to Tipton as Albion won the Cup by 3 goals to 2.

One of the largest council developments in the 1930s was the Tibbington Estate, which acquired the local nickname 'Abyssinia'. Its main thoroughfare was Central Avenue seen here in the late 1960s from the embankment which carried the Old Main Line canal until its abandonment in the 1950s. The houses on the right, as well as those in the adjacent Elm Crescent, suffered from subsidence and were demolished in the early 1990s. The site was redeveloped as the Walker Grange residential home, opened on 27 February 1992 and named in honour of local councillor Ted Walker.

THE BLACK COUNTRY SOCIETY

This voluntary society, affiliated to the Civic Trust, was founded in 1967 as a reaction to the trend of the late 1950s and early 1960s to amalgamate everything into large units and in the Midlands to sweep away the area's industrial heritage in the process.

The general aim of the Society is to create interest in the past, present and future of the Black Country, and early on it campaigned for the establishment of an industrial museum. In 1975 the Black Country Living Museum was started by Dudley Borough Council on 26 acres of totally derelict land adjoining the grounds of Dudley Castle. This has developed into an award-winning museum which attracts over 250,000 visitors annually.

In 1998 the Museum Board secured a lottery grant of nearly £3 million towards the £4.5 million cost of building a state-of-the-art interpretation centre. Known as the Rolfe Street Baths Project as it incorporated that Smethwick building which was transferred to the museum site, it was officially opened on 18 May 2001. It includes two fine exhibition halls, administration and storage rooms and retains the original Victorian building's façade. The museum's already wide range of attractions is likely soon to be increased in the field of transport with the acquisition of two major collections of vehicles.

At the Black Country Living Museum there is a boat dock fully equipped to restore narrowboats of wood and iron and different vessels can be seen on the dock throughout the year. From behind the Bottle and Glass Inn visitors can travel on a canal boat into Dudley Canal Tunnel, a memorable journey to see spectacular limestone caverns and the fascinating Castle Mill Basin.

There are 2,650 members of the Black Country Society and all receive the quarterly magazine *The Blackcountryman*, of which 136 issues have been published since its founding in 1967. In the whole collection there are some 2,000 authoritative articles on all aspects of the Black Country by historians, teachers, researchers, students, subject experts and ordinary folk with an extraordinary story to tell. The whole constitutes a unique resource about the area and is a mine of information for students and researchers who frequently refer to it. Many schools and libraries are subscribers. Over 3,300 copies of the magazine are printed each quarter. It is non-commercial, and contributors do not receive payment for their articles.

PO Box 71 · Kingswinford · West Midlands DY6 9YN